Able Muse Anthology

Praise for the *Able Muse Anthology*

Over the last twelve years, Able Muse and its extraordinary companion website the *Eratosphere* have created a huge and influential virtual literary community. There is no better example of the New Bohemia of electronic culture. Poets, translators, critics, teachers, and readers gather in this vast, smokey virtual all-night cafe, sharing work, debating issues, providing advice and instruction. The clientele of the *Eratosphere* range from major poets to rank amateurs, all conversing as equals. There is no question that this invisible institution has become central to countless poets and critics, especially those interested in form and narrative, who find here an informed and engaged community impossible to surpass in the bricks and mortar world. Able Muse has now gathered the best of their works in both prose and verse in an ink-and-paper anthology. This book fills an important gap in understanding what is really happening in early twenty-first century American poetry.

— **Dana Gioia**

This extraordinarily rich collection of fiction, poetry, essays and art by so many gifted enablers of the Muse is both a present satisfaction and a promise of future performance. May this now decade-old enterprise continue to flourish!

— **Charles Martin**

Neither unskilled, lethargic, nor distracted from their proper enterprise, the muses in the past decade have been singularly able, as this outstanding anthology of work from the *Able Muse* demonstrates. The poems, including fine work by R.S. Gwynn, Mark Jarman, X.J. Kennedy, Leslie Monsour, Timothy Steele, Alan Sullivan, Diane Thiel, Deborah Warren, and a score of other skilled poets, almost define what good American poetry is and should be, whether in traditional rhymed forms, which dominate here, or freer ones. Marvelous wit appears throughout. Translations from three languages, an interview with Steele, and good essays on rhyme, Richard Wilbur, and Turner Cassity provide reinforcement for the high poetic values on display. Short fiction, artistic photographs, and other artwork—some almost surrealistic—add contrasting notes to a collection that is not just pleasing but *important* as an artistic statement, a "defense and illustration" of poetry today.

— **Catharine Savage-Brosman**

You hold in your hands a remarkable anthology of poems, translations, an interview, essays, short stories and visual art. These represent the best of the *Able Muse*, an on-line magazine now defying current trends by moving into print. To have this work published between covers is to meet not only such well-known writers as X.J. Kennedy, Rachel Hadas, R.S. Gwynn and A.E. Stallings, but also to form an acquaintance with a much larger community, including writers who will be new to you but who share both devotion and accomplishment. These poems do not present form for form's sake; they are lively and engaged works of art. The interview with Timothy Steele; the essays on formal practice, Richard Wilbur and the late Turner Cassity; the stories long and short; the striking range of visual art all lend this book a broader interest than any other anthology you are likely to encounter. Welcome to the dexterous makers of the *Able Muse*.

— **David Mason**

Much so-called poetry you can read on the web merits an epithet coined by John Updike—"road kill on the information highway." But *Able Muse* for more than a decade has been a reliable source of the real thing. Two dozen of my favorite metrical poets illuminate this splendid anthology, besides others I'm grateful to meet. Here's a generous serving of the cream of *Able Muse*, including not only formal verse but nonmetrical work that also displays careful craft, memorable fiction (seven remarkable stories), striking artwork and photography, and incisive critical prose (don't miss Susanne J. Doyle's funny, heart-warming memoir of Turner Cassity). As this enjoyable selection proves, editor Alex Pepple has enlisted more than his share of the best art and writing America has generated lately.

— **X.J. Kennedy**

Able Muse Anthology

Best of the first decade of poetry, fiction, nonfiction and art

Edited by Alexander Pepple
Foreword by Timothy Steele

ABLE MUSE PRESS

Able Muse Press

www.ablemusepress.com

ISBN 978-0-9865338-0-8

Able Muse Press is an imprint of *Able Muse*—a review of poetry, prose and art—at
www.ablemuse.com

Eratosphere is an online literary workshop for poetry, prose and art sponsored by *Able Muse*
at http://eratosphere.ablemuse.com

Heartfelt thanks to our proofreaders extraordinaire: Julie Stoner, Gregory Dowling and Tim Love.

Able Muse Press
467 Saratoga Avenue #602
San Jose, CA 95129

CONTENTS

INTERVIEWS

POETRY TRANSLATION

POETRY

ART & PHOTOGRAPHY

Timothy Steele is the author of four collections of poetry: *Uncertainties and Rest* (1979), *Sapphics against Anger and Other Poems* (1986), *The Color Wheel* (Johns Hopkins University Press, 1994), and *Toward the Winter Solstice* (Swallow Press/ Ohio University Press, 2006). The first two were reprinted in 1995 as a joint volume, *Sapphics and Uncertainties: Poems 1970-1986* (University of Arkansas Press, 1995). His two books of literary criticism and scholarship are *Missing Measures: Modern Poetry and the Revolt against Meter* (University of Arkansas Press, 1990) and *All the Fun's in How You Say a Thing: An Explanation of Meter and Versification* (Ohio University Press, 1999). He has also edited *The Poems of J. V. Cunningham* (Swallow Press/Ohio University Press, 1997).

Steele's honors include a Guggenheim Fellowship, a Peter I. B. Lavan Younger Poets Award from the Academy of American Poets, the Los Angeles PEN Center's Literary Award for Poetry, a California Arts Council Grant, a Commonwealth Club of California Medal for Poetry, and the Robert Fitzgerald Award for Excellence in the Study of Prosody. Born in Burlington, Vermont, in 1948, Steele lives with his wife in Los Angeles and is a professor of English at California State University, Los Angeles.

Timothy Steele

Foreword

When Alex Pepple posted the first issue of the *Able Muse* in 1999, he wrote in his editorial statement of purpose, "Despite the plethora of online journals covering a wide spectrum of literary interests, most of the poetry published on the web has been free verse. . . . So, this formalist set out to tip the balance a little the other way." Eleven years later, few would dispute his success in achieving his goal. Under Pepple's direction, the *Able Muse* has featured, on a site that is beautifully designed and easy to navigate, a lively mixture of verse, prose, and visual art in various forms. Meanwhile, *Eratosphere*, the journal's forum of discussion groups, has offered its members (who now number over 6,000) the chance to participate in writing workshops and to exchange ideas on a broad range of literary topics. But most of all, the magazine has focused on metrical poetry, publishing new work by both seasoned practitioners and excellent younger writers. If *The Formalist* and its successor *Measure* have proved the chief print organs in the United States for contemporary metered verse, if The West Chester University Poetry Conference has fulfilled the same function among literary symposia, the *Able Muse* has become the premiere online resource for those interested in current work that employs the time-tested tools of the poetic trade.

The present anthology reprints a generous selection from the materials the *Able Muse* has published to date; and the volume provides, among other things, a chance to reflect on the aesthetic energies and faith that have fueled the magazine. When, a century ago, such early masters of free verse as Ezra Pound, T.S. Eliot, and William Carlos Williams challenged and dismantled traditional metric, they hoped that their enterprise would lead to a new prosody as coherent, harmonious, and shareable as the systems of the past had been. In the generations that followed, free verse became an autonomous and vital genre of poetry, and poets so widely adopted it that it largely eclipsed metrical verse. But a new metric never materialized. Instead of undergoing prosodic consolidation, free verse ramified, from decade to decade, into increasingly numerous and divergent paths and modes.

From our vantage now, we can see why hopes for a new metric were disappointed. Meters emerge from and reflect the phonetic and grammatical structures of the languages they serve. Sometimes these basic structures change—as was the case, for example, in late antiquity, when stress replaced length as a salient feature of European speech and when meters based on accent and/or fixed syllable count eventually supplanted the quantitative meters of classical poetry. (Another such transformation occurred in the wake of the Norman Conquest, when, along with other developments, the flexional forms of Old English broke down under the influence of French, and the largely falling rhythms of Anglo-Saxon prosody gave way to the principally rising rhythms of Middle and Modern English verse.) However, such changes cannot be wished into being or willfully imposed on speech. They require fundamental shifts in the linguistic conditions of languages. Absent these, radical prosodic experiments may well produce singular and miscellaneous exercises of great interest; but they are unlikely to lead to the discovery or creation of comprehensively useful models of rhythm.

Regarded in this light, the effort today to recover meter is not a protest against free verse but a recognition that it cannot, whatever its virtues, serve as a substitute for the art of rhythmically organized speech. To be sure, some have suggested that this metrical renaissance expresses, in the phrase of one authority, "a dangerous nostalgia"—a longing for some sort of Good Old Days of Poetry. Yet contemporary metrical poets engage, no less than do contemporary writers in other media, the subjects and experiences of their times. If some poets have returned to meter, they have done so because the medium gives them access to telling rhythm, precision of statement, imagistic focus, and that enchanting fusion of order and variety that has always been the essence of fine versification. And if any philosophical belief unites such poets, it is perhaps merely that meter has served our species valuably throughout its literary history and that it would be tragically wasteful to do away with it or let it die. It would make as much sense to do away with prose.

Whatever the future holds, we can celebrate in the present Alex Pepple's realization of his original vision. May the *Able Muse* continue to offer stimulating translations, essays, book reviews, prose fiction, verse (metrical and free), festschriften, interviews, and artwork. May *Eratosphere* continue to host spirited colloquia and workshops. And may this retrospective anthology prove to be only the first of many such volumes that document the journal's rich and ongoing contributions to our cultural life.

Alexander Pepple is an electrical engineer who has worked and consulted with several heavyweight high-tech companies . . . and a few lightweights. His poems have appeared or will appear in *La Petite Zine, Eclectica, Snakeskin, Octavo, The Melic Review, Light Quarterly, San Pedro River Review* and elsewhere. He is the editor of the online and print journal, *Able Muse,* and the founder of the related *Eratosphere* online workshop.

Alexander Pepple

Introduction

The *Able Muse Anthology* celebrates *Able Muse*'s journey through its first decade and beyond, by showcasing the best of the published poetry, fiction, essays, interviews, book reviews, art and photography. It was a delightful decade of online publishing at *Able Muse*—I dare say, the first of many more to follow. This anthology is in some ways a bridge to the forthcoming periodical print version of the journal, with the online version becoming supplemental.

The *Able Muse Anthology* brings you poetry and fiction from established and emerging poets and writers, complemented by essays, reviews, art and photography. It includes work from Mark Jarman, Rachel Hadas, Turner Cassity, Stephen Edgar, R.S. Gwynn, Timothy Steele, Rhina P. Espaillat, A.M. Juster, Geoffrey Brock, Timothy Murphy, Jennifer Reeser, Beth Houston, Annie Finch, Dick Davis, X.J. Kennedy, A.E. Stallings, Richard Moore, Richard Wakefield, Julie Kane, Alan Sullivan, Chelsea Rathburn, Kim Bridgford, Deborah Warren, Diane Thiel, Rose Kelleher, Leslie Monsour, Lyn Lifshin, Amit Majmudar, Richard Wakefield, Marilyn L. Taylor, Len Krisak, Dolores Hayden, Thaisa Frank, Dennis Must, Soliaire Miles, Misha Gordin, and several others. This list includes several *Eratosphere* members.

The success of *Able Muse* has been gratifying, exceeding the expectations I had in mind when it was launched in 1999. Back then, we were the first and only online journal devoted to metrical poetry. A decade later, we have inspired a wide array of like journals that focus on metrical poetry in one form or another—such as sonnets only, women only, nonce forms, and so on. May they all thrive in their chosen niches and beyond! Today's *Able Muse* has evolved to allow an expanded focus that includes a few exceptional free verse poems and fiction from established and emerging writers, along with essays, reviews and art.

In tandem with *Eratosphere* (*Able Muse*'s online forums and literary workshop), we've played a major role in the seasoning of some of the best metricists writing today. Indeed, we'd like to think that we played a major role in the wider acceptance and publication of metrical poetry by mainstream print and online journals. *Eratosphere* members are among the best poets writing and getting published today. Several are represented in this anthology. It includes the work of A.M. Juster, *Eratosphere*'s very first moderator, as well as that of other current and past moderators such as A.E. Stallings, Alan Sullivan, Timothy Murphy, Deborah Warren, Richard Wakefield, R.S. Gwynn, Marilyn L. Taylor, Jennifer Reeser, John Beaton, Catherine Chandler and Maryann Corbett.

Able Muse started with the Premiere Issue in the latter part of 1999 (www.ablemuse.com/index-premiere.html retains the full archives). We premiered with stunning black and white conceptual photography from Featured Artist Misha Gordin. The Featured Poet was the prolific Beth Houston, who brought us work dominated by ekphrastic sonnets based on mythology and the scriptures. Her contribution included an acclaimed sonnet e-book that became widely viewed, and even pirated by high-end archival sites asking for payment to access what we've always provided free of charge. But that's another story.

The Millennial Issue straddled the big event of the time—Y2K—and thus was saturated with related news and hyped fears, especially, about computers and the Internet . . . fears which proved overstated when the time came. There was some play on this with Randy Adam's Grave Millennium photo series. (The issue is archived at www.ablemuse.com/index-2k.html). It featured Kamil Varga's staged photography and the finely crafted poetry of Leslie Monsour, the Featured Poet. This was the first issue in which we started publishing fiction and brought you stories from Thaisa Frank, Alan Cheuse and others.

The Symposium Issue saw the return of Misha Gordin's conceptual photography and featured encaustics and collage artwork from local artist Linda Spencer, who was based in California's Silicon Valley at the time. There was fiction from Dennis Must, Nan Leslie and others. For the first and only time, we did not have a featured poet, but rather a panel of featured poets. They participated in an online symposium I'd set up for them, fueled by the dynamics of the West Chester poetry conference that year. The panel consisted of Rachel Hadas, Mark Jarman, A.E. Stallings, R.S. Gwynn and Diane Thiel. (The Symposium Issue archives can be found at www.ablemuse.com/index-v3.html.)

The Community Issue (archived at www.ablemuse.com/index-v4.html) featured Diane Fenster's digital artwork, including her notable Waste Land series portraying characters from the T.S. Eliot poem. There were also the digital hyper photos of Jochen Brennecke. We featured Len Krisak's poetry and his conversation with Rhina P. Espaillat. The issue presented the winners of the first Tipsy Muse Light Verse Competition (held at *Eratosphere* with contest judge A.E. Stallings) and the *Eratosphere* Poet Contest (with judge Timothy Steele).

The Critical Issue, one of our leanest (at www.ablemuse.com/index-v5.html), featured poetry from Annie Finch and her interview by R.S. Gwynn. There was also a wonderful group of poems from Dolores Hayden.

After the Critical Issue, *Able Muse* went into a long hiatus—coincident with Silicon Valley's (and the worldwide) economic downturn . . . coincident with the disappearance of the day job of the sole sponsor of the *Able Muse* publication efforts! Despite that setback, *Eratosphere* continued to thrive and took on a life of its own as a most important and highly popular literary forum on the World Wide Web. And I stress worldwide, which is the scope of *Eratosphere*.

Able Muse did rise again. Our last three and most recent issues represented in this anthology, starting with the Reload Issue (archives at www.ablemuse.com/cover/index.php), breathed new life into *Able Muse*, both in the upgraded publication infrastructure based on the newer Web 2.0 technologies and the automated content management tools. In particular, there was strong featured poetry from Geoffrey Brock. We began including not just audio readings—as we'd done from the very first issue of *Able Muse*—but also video reading for poets and writers who could provide it. There was, for the first time, a Featured Artist and Musician—Solitaire Miles, with a showcase of her artwork and jazz vocals. We also added a new Spotlight Poet section with Alan Sullivan as the first poet in that role, including his conversation with Timothy Murphy.

Sadly, just one day before going to print with this anthology, we received the devastating news that Alan Sullivan had passed away after his long and courageous battle with leukemia. He was a fine poet who contributed immensely to *Eratosphere* as one of our first moderators—an *Eratosphere* stalwart whose critique and mentorship on the Deep End poetry workshop *is* legendary. He is already greatly missed.

Since the Reload Issue, *Able Muse* has settled into a consistent semiannual publication schedule. In the Workshops Issue that followed, we showcased the talent from our online workshop, *Eratosphere*, starting with our Featured Poet Jennifer Reeser, a participant and former moderator. (This issue is archived at www.ablemuse.com/v7/cover/index.html.) There was also spotlight poetry from Catherine Chandler, another *Eratosphere* participant and former moderator. The artwork came mostly from *Eratosphere*'s art forum regulars, notably, Terri Graham, the joint Featured Artist with Andrew Dolphin.

The Tribute Issue that followed was our first dedication issue, with a section devoted to celebrating the life and work of the late Turner Cassity, who passed away when we began putting the issue together (archived at www.ablemuse.com/v8/cover/index.html). This included some of his new, previously unpublished poetry and an accompanying video reading. There were of course the regular and usual sections, with Featured Poet Stephen Edgar, Spotlight Poet John Beaton, and Featured Artist Royena Rasnat (who brought us stunning images and artwork from her native Bangladesh).

The final issue represented in this anthology is the Volta Issue (archived at www.ablemuse.com/v9/cover/index.html), marking a turning point after which we'll begin publishing a print version of *Able Muse* in conjunction with online previews and samples. In this issue—forthcoming at the time of writing this introduction—we include the work of Featured Poet Rose Kelleher, Spotlight Poet Shekhar Aiyar, and Featured Artists Sara G. Umemoto and Billy Monday.

This anthology—the distillation of the best of the best poems, fiction, essays, reviews, art and photography previously published in *Able Muse*'s first ten years—brings you work as good as you'll find anywhere. We hope that you'll be edified, entertained and intellectually challenged and stimulated by it. We hope that you will enjoy reading and viewing the *Able Muse Anthology* as much as we have enjoyed bringing it to you in our journey through the last decade and beyond.

Able Muse Anthology

Best of the first decade of poetry, fiction, nonfiction and art

Brian Culhane

Philosopher's Wool

Some alchemists called [burned zinc] *lana philosophica*, Latin for "philosopher's wool," because it collected in wooly tufts, while others thought it looked like white snow and named it *ninx album*.

—*Wikipedia, "Zinc"*

Eager alchemists
Shaking stubborn fists
At the universe
Often made things worse
For those standing by
Whose astonished cry
Could be heard through walls
As black smoke filled halls:
Is this truly wise?
What if someone dies?!
An unholy blast
Might expunge the past
When flame touched cow's blood,
Saltpeter and mud,
Or burned base metal
In an old kettle
Until the whole room
Stank of common doom,
Of unwashed sinners
(Mere rank beginners)
Stumbling ahead
With incautious tread
On the littered floor
Where, amid the gore,
Truth was said to lie
Waiting for some dye
To imbue with gold

1

(As writers of old
Had said would happen)
Ordinary men.
Surely, it was thought,
Wealth was what art brought
To occult research.
From Minerva's perch
The owl flies aslant,
Though we think it can't,
And must hit the mark
Even in the dark.
So in alchemy
The learned set free
In a certain flame
What is zinc by name
("Philosopher's wool"
In an ancient school),
As such metal learns
Flight by what it burns
And drizzles down white
If the timing's right.

A history of zinc
Hardly makes us think,
Except by way of
Likenesses to love,
Which, when heated, too
Becomes something new
As it changes shape
Under magic's cape.
Once zinc turns to snow,
Its flight up will show
Heights lovers may fall
Should they, after all,
Succumb to that state—
A precipitate,
An alloy of pain,
A chalky gray stain—

Which whitens with flakes
What it most mistakes
To be kindred hate.
Interanimate,
Love and hate obey,
Through this very day,
Laws that come from high;
Centuries go by
And still we fail,
Still mix the pail
Of our desire,
Still look in fire
For crucible's gold,
Though we cannot hold
Nature to account
For the wrong amount
If gold becomes zinc
And the missing link
Is thus missed again
In a dirty rain.
Zinc is wool, we're told.
So let love be gold,
Elusive at best
Or a kind of test
Whose secret's best kept
When salt rain is wept.

Shekhar Aiyar

Biography of a Sword

The scimitar behind the glass
lies naked on its velvet bed.
A placard estimates its mass
but leaves the body count unsaid.

A general held it, then a king.
Impartially it did their will
with blade and pommel, lunge and swing.
Its legend waxed from kill to kill.

Promoted to a metaphor,
its aspect changed; the palmworn hilt
grew diamonds, and the scars it wore
surrendered to a coat of gilt.

And now it sleeps through whispered praise
and grave appraisals of its worth:
a ploughshare dreaming of the days
it signed its name in famished earth.

Shekhar Aiyar

Diary of a Tourist

Connaught Place Market, New Delhi

Outside the window, in the pillared shade
a woman kneels and shakes a coffee can
at noon's detritus. By my count she's made
no more than two rupees since I began
to sip my first latté an hour ago.
The boy beside her reads the sun's progress
with practised eyes, and grimaces as though
he's only at her side under duress.

It's late. I should be elsewhere, but allow
a last refill, and sit behind the pane
a moment more. The heat is peaking now.
The boy flops down and won't sit up again.
She strokes his cheek, and bends as if to say
that people will not always be this way.

Rhina P. Espaillat

My Father's Coins

My father's coins: they signal where he never
lived to travel, but perhaps had meant
to go, or longed to go, since duties sever
desire from both fruition and intent.

Look, this is threepence: George the Sixth in profile,
with thistles on the obverse; here, the beak
of Mexico clasping a serpent, guile
seized by winged force; here, *République*

Française haloes a maiden laurel-crowned.
And where's this champion riding, lance in place
for combat, horse's hooves on holy ground
and one proud word, *España?* This stern face

is José Artigas, who fought Spain for Uruguay
and died imprisoned by the French. What thoughts
must have blown through my father's hours, like high
and distant flutes! His careful figures, noughts

rounded Palmer-style, all double-checked,
kept errors out and always reconciled
to the last penny, every sum correct,
expenses paid, frail wife and his one child

provided for. But on the credit side,
what was he left with for his voyages
unmade, unspoken dreams unsatisfied?
A sense of having done it well, and yes,

love, that most fluid currency of all
whose coin is valid everywhere, the stuff
of which real wealth is made. I know he'd call
that true. One wants to think it was enough.

6

Geoffrey Brock

Shades of Tucson: 2005

I have two trees in my front yard. Jesús,
my next-door neighbor, told me yesterday
I ought to cut the chinaberry down:
non-native, he said. The other, a eucalyptus,

was planted fifty years ago by James,
who grew up in this house, though he now lives
across the street, next door to Mrs. Chávez,
whose husband (James once told me) tried to drive

James' parents from the neighborhood because
(a) they were black and (b) they had two sons—
while Chávez had two daughters. This took place
when 13th St. was dirt and the president

Eisenhower. Chávez died of cancer
twenty years back, and every morning now
I drink my Earl Grey on my porch, which once
was James's porch, in eucalyptus shade,

and watch as James goes out his gate and in
the Chávez gate: he brings her paper up,
waters her plants, does little things she can't.
God ought to give him something grand for that—

a ticket to heaven at least. But then again
perhaps such deeds repay themselves somehow;
perhaps each daily kindness to the widow
feels like a scoop of dirt on the past's grave.

I turned from chinaberry to eucalyptus
and said: that one's not native either, is it?
No, said Jesús, but this is Tucson, bro,
a person can't give up that kind of shade.

Kate Benedict

Glimpses of the Body at a City Window

Mine is not a building with a river view.
No park outside my window changes hue
with the successive seasons. If I crane,
I see chaotic traffic, and a fire lane.

Shades shield me from the urban mess.
If now and then I raise them, it's to guess
the weather, not to linger at the sill.
Still, one day I lingered against my will.

Across the street, I saw a man, a very
old man, naked in his room. A terry
towel—gray, perhaps once white—glided past
his hips. He bent, and his momentous ass

hovered above the avenue. Vast, pink—
he bore his great weight gently to the brink
of that too public sill. His wife helped him dress.
He put up with each capable caress.

Were they not mindful of the spectacle
they made, he in his enormous shackle
of slack skin, she in her intimate act
of wifely duty? Their street-show lacked

self-consciousness or shame. Uninhibited
as infants, pure, free, they exhibited
his old exquisite body and were proud.
It wouldn't have surprised me, had they bowed.

Nor did it surprise me when the scene would play
again on other days, or that I'd stay
by the window, riveted to the floor,
or that in time their figures came no more.

Charles Baudelaire

Harmony of Evening

Here coming is the time when on its stem will blow
Each flower, like a censer, now evaporating.
The sounds and the perfumes turn in the air of evening,
A melancholy waltz and languid vertigo!

Each flower, like a censer, now evaporating,
The violin is quivering like a heart in woe,
A melancholy waltz and languid vertigo!
The sky is sad and lovely, like a great repose.

The violin is quivering like a heart in woe,
A tender heart, which hates vast, black oblivion!
The sky is sad and lovely, like a great repose.
The sun is drowned in its own blood which thickens.

A tender heart which hates vast, black oblivion
Collects all vestiges from bygone luminance!
The sun is drowned in its own blood which thickens . . .
Your remembrance shone within me like a monstrance!

— *Translated from the French of Charles Baudelaire*
   by Jennifer Reeser

9

Turner Cassity

Mej. Zelle

In youth I was your basic overweight Dutch frump,
As at the end I was. Between, the quantum jump

To Mata Hari, ethnic artist dancing nude
Before Crowned Heads, if not the Asian multitude

That would know bump-and-grinding when they saw it. Spy?
Well, maybe. Such few secrets as I could supply

I hardly understood. But faced with firing squad
I was as firm as Nurse Cavell. A simple nod

That signals one is ready; and the blindfold off,
To serve as scarf, inhibit any final cough.

Once dead, I enter into glamour. Who can see
A Garbo playing starchy Edith and not me?

And if I danced enticing, Indo-Minsky scenes,
They were my income. Nurse Cavell had private means.

Turner Cassity

Edith Cavell

England's recruiting poster Joan of Arc,
I was a crypto-Walloon, and a stark

Reminder that when all is said and done
The letter of the law was with the Hun,

Although I rose at once to such renown
As was the Lusitania's, once down,

If with as little claim to innocence.
All that could be brought forth in my defense

Is that I did not profit from my acts,
And that confession is what guile exacts.

Do not think my examiners were fools,
Or did not judge according to their rules.

It is the rules I fault, and though in days
To come I may be seen as through a blaze

Of Union Jacks and poppies, do I fail
If, unlike fearless Florence Nightingale

Shaking the military in her zeal
To bring the male establishment to heel,

I'm seen as only fragile victim-nurse,
Or I-Want-You in posters, which is worse?

I'd sooner I urged Flemings to revolt
Or pacifists in Government to bolt.

Out in the Empire I gave name to streets,
But that was pre-Mahatma. Time deletes.

Cally Conan-Davies

The Great Ocean Road

A hot-wired spirit sparking in the rain,
you jolted me to life, unfroze my heart,
and all my tangled currents you'd explain
as if you read my bathymetric chart.
We ran with leaf-shaped boards into the sea,
birds wheeling, wave noise tossing up white spray;
I dived, holding your breath, and learnt to breathe
on southern coasts where fire and water play.

Your face, creased like a map of what we've seen,
the reefs and tree ferns, lines of glassy waves,
is proof the outside world reflects within
and sculpts our ends as green seas carve out caves.

Sometimes at dusk the humpbacked ocean slows,
and even thoughts like these have undertows.

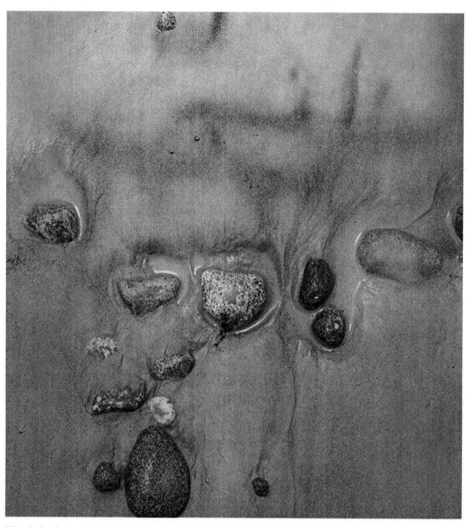

Terri Graham (Undercurrent)

Terri Graham (Her Mother Called Her Ivy)

Catherine Chandler

Drought

Above our field of stunted corn and thistle,
a lone chimango circles, scouts, homes in
as sure and swift and savage as a missile,
pins down a leveret, rips away its skin,

ignores the terror-stricken eyes, the squeal,
devours the pulsing heart. His thirst now slaked,
he leaves the rest for a carancho's meal.
The land is quivering, crumbling, cracked and caked,

the stream a silent checkerboard of mud,
the well near dry. I pray this lack of water
won't leave me stony at the sight of blood,
of rational, inexorable slaughter.

(Saladillo, Argentina, 2009)

Catherine Chandler

Supernova

A burnished afternoon. Why dull it with
a lapse to metaphor
or scientific fact, or myth,
or say there's more

to life than what the naked eye perceives
or what the ear can hear?
Why paraphrase the shhhhing leaves,
the swoosh of deer?

Why try to parse the chirrup of the birds
or posit love's a stew
of enzymes? Why resort to words
when hush will do?

As afternoon declines to dusk I stand
uncertain and perplexed,
your ashes in my trembling hand.
I ask, What next?

Then grant the constancy of truths and laws,
of motive, meaning, mind;
of logic, reason, purpose, cause;
because I find

it's easier to release you, as I must,
less harrowing by far,
knowing that all human dust
was once a star.

Andrew Dolphin (Chi)

Suzanne J. Doyle

Laying It on the Line for Turner Cassity
(1929-2009)

What I miss most about Turner Cassity is sitting next to him, listening to the mesmerizing cadence of his aristocratic, southern Mississippian accent. Whether he was narrating his latest travel adventure, critically appraising the work of another poet, or wittily skewering any pompous, dishonest person, his words fell soft and delicious. In addition to being a master of the art of conversation, Turner was also always a gentleman—polite, gracious, precisely barbered, and well-dressed. Frankly, he was the best date I ever had. Ever. One Decatur evening in 1989 stands out in particular, or, I should say, parts of it, because some parts are a wee bit blurry.

Whenever we planned a night on the town, Turner would tempt me with, "Come on, Suzanne, let's be *wicked* together." A good part of being "wicked" included gin and the effervescent tonic of gossip. (See "Page from a Bar Guide" for his paean to gin.) But that night in Decatur began differently. It started with a walk to a bar that was simply a clean, well-lighted place. A room filled with tables. It might have been a VFW hall. There was nothing memorable about it. It was there, however, that Turner introduced me to a cocktail I'll never forget: the French 77.

By the book, the French 77 consists of a shot of elderberry liqueur and lemon juice in a flute, with the flute then filled with champagne. But the way the bartender made this drink for Turner, whom he had surely served before, was to present him with what I remember as being a beaker of champagne and a shot of cognac. Turner sank the shot in the champers. I have a clear memory of the shot slowly rocking its way to the bottom, like the depth-charge it surely was. If I'd even tasted that drink, I'm sure the rest of the evening would be a complete blank. Turner had two. (I've tried and tried to edit that chemistry beaker from memory, but it just won't go away. So I've concluded it must have been there.)

From Decatur we drove to the Ritz-Carlton Buckhead, where we had dinner in The Dining Room. The Dining Room's decor was plush upholstered banquettes, flocked wallpaper, sconces, reproductions of paintings of blood-lined horses, heavy drapes—Tara redecorated by Scarlet on Prozac. Turner may have said something about forgetting his riding crop. Or maybe it was the 25-year difference in our ages that prompted the *maître d'* to seat us in a dark booth at a far corner of the room. He was wise. What ensued was Rabelaisian. A 1982 Chateau Talbot was involved, as were quail served in more than one way. I distinctly remember the crunching of tiny bird bones, a fact confirmed two weeks later when the mail delivered Turner's recipe for Quail Roasted in Vermouth. It was a photocopied page from a cookbook, with the instructions annotated in his unmistakable, precise, left-slanting block print, assuring me of his recipe's superiority.

After the quail, the game continued: venison and rabbit. That's right, Bambi and Thumper down the hatch without remorse. For dessert we were to share a chocolate soufflé ordered at the start of the meal. By the time it arrived, I was stuffed. But there was nothing small about Turner's appetite. Magically, the soufflé disappeared. Surely a digestif was called for. During which the conversation turned to: why not have a child together? We picked a name. That was fun! And the last thing ever said on the subject. I wish I could tell you the name we settled on, but even I am not that irreverent.

The evening was still young. Turner promised me a piano bar and piloted us back to Decatur in what was a riverboat of a car, no, a Riverboat Queen of a car. I don't think either one of us could actually see past the hood, it was so long and sleek, so heavily encrusted with chrome, so very V8. Earlier in the evening he had pointed out with glee: no seat belts! Having inherited the car from a cousin, he was surprised to find it even fit in his garage.

We parked at a juke joint next to the railroad tracks. It was a shack really. The walls were rough board, no paint. There was no bar per se, just a table set with bottles and glasses. But in the center of the room, as promised: a piano. It was not grand but upright. The piano player, unfortunately, was not. He lay blacked-out over a table in the corner. Even we could tell the party was over. I tottered back to the car in high heels across what felt like a bed of cinders, leaning heavily on Turner's arm for support. The next day when I called him before leaving for the airport Turner provided perfect closure by saying, "Suzanne, that was a Pearl Harbor of the mind."

I don't know anyone who would disagree with Helen Trimpi in *Stanford Magazine* when she said, "He is the most witty man in conversation I've ever known." It's a fact that is documented repeatedly, for instance by anecdotes in the *Emory Wheel* article covering the memorial service held at Emory University's Woodruff Library, and in Memye Curtis Tucker's memoir[1]. At poetry readings, for example, he often announced variants on the line: "I write about the wickedness of the world—that way I'll never run out of material." I wish there were dozens more reminiscences to commemorate Turner's life in conversation, and hope the future will bring forth many. Of course, his ferocious wit and gentle wisdom are immortalized in the thousands of letters sent to friends and family, but he expressly prohibited their publication. Fortunately, because he was such a prolific poet, we can turn to his work for more of the man we loved and admired as friend, teacher, and poet. And, despite his protestation at readings that he never wrote about his own emotions, the poems often prove otherwise, as he pens in "He Whom Ye Seek:"

> . . . "He is not here?"
> He is, however. He is every single share,
> Knife, fork, and spoon. I am the blood the portraits were,
> Those carats, iambs, trips. All of my life is here.

According to Bob Barth, Turner's literary executor, there was, in fact, a fat envelope of poems in a safe deposit box in Jackson, Mississippi (and silver cutlery in another). Specifically, that envelope contained all the new poems Turner published in *The Destructive Element: New and Selected Poems*[2]. Bob also discovered on Turner's personal computer more than a gigabyte (that is an enormous number of text files!) of unpublished work. He is currently in the process of reading and organizing that work into books and chapbooks.

One whole book, entitled simply *New Book* by Turner, had already been assembled, including a table of contents. The trove of unpublished work also includes book-length poems. Those who are familiar with Turner's work, such as his *Silver Out of Shanghai*, will recognize these as a specialty of his. We are lucky enough to offer here several of the unpublished poems, courtesy of Bob. They remind me again of how brilliant Turner was at dramatic monologue. I was also reminded of how brilliant he was at blank verse dramatic dialogue when reading his posthumously published chapbook from Scienter

---

[1] Editor's Note: Published in the [Turner Cassity] Tribute issue of *Able Muse*, December 2009, available online at www.ablemuse.com/v8/index.html.
[2] As told to me by Bob Barth in phone conversation September 27, 2009.

Press: *Under Two Flags: Echoes of the Foreign Legion.* From the ribald reminiscences of two geriatric legionnaires in Rhodesia, to a bizarre confrontation of strangers in midland Texas over a cooler containing cottonmouths and a wheel of brie, the two medium-length poems that make up this volume are Turner at his most arch.

But I digress. Back to the unpublished work. Of most interest to me are two chapbook-length collections of poems under the title of *Poems for Isobel.* These are poems that deal openly with the subject of being a gay man. They are to my mind among Turner's best work. But why, you may wonder as I did, were they for Isobel?

I have to thank Bob Barth for solving the mystery. He remembered Turner's poem "A Word from Isobel," a dramatic monologue spoken by Isabel Burton, wife of Sir Richard Francis Burton, the 19th-century explorer and poet responsible for bringing unexpurgated texts, including *One Thousand and One Nights* and the *Kama Sutra*, to the English speaking world. After his death, Burton's wife Isabel destroyed his translation of *The Perfumed Garden,* the better part of which was a chapter, usually omitted in later translations, on pederasty. Burton had included extensive and comprehensive notes on the subject. Turner's dedication of his gay poems to Isobel might be interpreted as thumbing his nose at her Catholic idea of saving her husband from eternal damnation by preventing others from being led into sin by his work. Or, Isobel may have been the vestigial Calvinist in Turner that kept the gay poems from publication and, perhaps, at times contemplated burning them. I think he raises and then answers the question himself in the following lines from "He Whom Ye Seek:"

> . . . was it a stunting or a growth?
> It was the risk of so much safety. It was both.

For years Turner and I had a running joke about the Isobel poems, although he never called them that. He simply referred to them as "The Porn." After he retired he said, "If I live to be 75 I'm going to take up smoking and publish the porn." For the next 10 years I'd beg, "I'm so bored without you. Send me the porn!" In August of 2000, shortly after one of his extended San Francisco visits, a plain manila envelope arrived addressed in Turner's signature hand. There was no question in my mind what it contained. Imagine my surprise to find only eight poems whose content was distinctly un-pornographic. True, they dealt with the life of gay bars and street hustlers, but there was nothing pornographic about them. Calling them "porn" had more to do with his southern Calvinistic upbringing and age than with their content.

What makes these poems stand out from much of Turner's work—which is often lapidary in structure and loaded with literary, historical, and geopolitical allusions—is how accessible they are. When I shared this observation with him, he replied, with not a little irony, "I guess I've finally learned that it's a gift to be simple." Which is not to say Turner's unmistakable voice does not come through loud and clear. Turner was always himself, even in gay bars, as illustrated below.

The Imp of the Perverse

The world is full of men whose dearest urge
Is sex with Quasimodo or the corpse
Of Alfred Douglas or with Eng and Chang,
Whose own dear urge may not have much to do
With hobbyists. (Well, Bosie's might have.) Seek
And ye shall find; God help you if you do.
The only worse outcome is to suspect
That they find you; that you are some construct
Outside normality. Hunchback, be off.
Lord Alfred, put on boxing gloves and try
Kickboxing with the freestyle Siamese.
Do not, I pray you, zero in on me.
I, neither item or collector, march
Always to the same drummer. Not, I add,
The Little Drummer Boy. I do not stalk.
Normality is the erotic point;
In what I am attracted to, that is.
Variety may be the spice of life,
But spices, you remember, came to be
From urgent need to hide the taste of rot.
Most hunting is for game already high.[3]

There is no despair like the despair a gay man or lesbian feels when surveying the patrons of a gay bar (at least in the old days) and realizing "Oh my God, this is the dating pool." And, if your 'erotic point is normality,' not only are the bars a desert of the heart, but you're probably set up to fall for a "straight" person. Trust me, I know, and so did Turner. He tackles the subject with a vengeance.

The Isobel poems also shed light on the subtext of many of the more personal of Turner's published poems, such as "Ways of Feeling," "The Strange Case of Dr. Jekyll and Dr. Jekyll," "Adding Rattles," "One of the Boys, or, Nothing Sad about My Captains," and "Open Wounds." I hope a publisher can be found to add Turner's take on gay life to the existing body of his published work. In particular, his perspective would stand in interesting contrast to Thom Gunn's.

I want to thank all of the poets who submitted work for this tribute[4]. Even in the submissions that didn't make it into the tribute, there were many lines that evoked Turner's enchanting personality and demonstrated deep appreciation of his work. I hope that as you read on you will enjoy the heroic march of Alicia Stallings couplets, the charming translations from the Persian by Dick Davis, Tim Steele's meditation on Nijinsky's tomb, Christophe Fricker's German translation of Turner's sizzling "Two are Four," Bill Conelly's elegy, Memye Tucker's reminiscence, and Helen Trimpi's video tribute. I believe Turner would have been touched by each and every one of these contributions. I know I was.

Turner's cousin said to him as he lay in hospital, days before his death, "When you get home, you'll have to write a poem about this." The seizure he'd suffered had robbed him of his ability to speak, but he managed to say, "I already have."[5] We won't ever get to hear that poem. But thanks to Kevin Durkin, who paid for production costs out of his own pocket, we can watch an excellent video of Turner reading at The Huntington Library in 2003. If you never met Turner, and even if you were lucky enough to have, this is a chance to see him at his best and hear his beautiful voice, that voice, buried forever in my heart.[6]

---

[4] Editor's Note: This refers to the Turner Cassity Tribute issue of *Able Muse*, December 2009, available online at www.ablemuse.com/v8/index.html.
[5] As told to me by Bob Barth in phone conversation September 27, 2009.
[6] Further Reading: *The New Georgia Encyclopedia*: "Turner Cassity" (www.georgiaencyclopedia.org/nge/Article.jsp?id=h-1254&hl=y).

Maryann Corbett

Long-Term Memory

His patience: that was what stunned us into silence.
His old intensity, but suddenly gentler,
the way he leaned into the conversation,
his eyes lit, his brows knitted a little.
And the care he gave the words—the names, the places,
details we'd never heard. The *paesan'* hands,
moving like swallows, as he labored to tell us
why he *must* leave: His parents needed him.
His father couldn't work—the rheumatism,
the fingers curled like claws, lying in the lap—
and barely any work to be had these days.
He was the oldest son. It was his duty.
His mother, in the hospital upstate,
just holding on. His boss at the CCC camp,
iron-fisted with the absentees.
And he had to keep that job, so he could get married.
He needed to leave tonight.
                         Did one of us speak?
I don't remember. Or did he catch a glimpse
of his own hands, knotted, ropey with veins,
or feel the uneven thinness of his hair
in his nervous fingering through it? Something shifted.
Some raveled nerve end touched, and in its spark
he saw: the parents who needed him were dead,
long dead; his promised bride was the shrunken woman
whose eyes clutched at him now; and every job
he'd built a self with, over seventy years,
was ash and air. We watched the knowledge settle,
pressing, the way it pressed down every night,
the decades dense as stone, crushing his face,
the lines at his eyes deepening like wounds,
until, again tonight, he was shaking his fists,
cursing, shouting, like the man we knew.

Daniel L. Corrie

Sloppiness or Vitality? —
Rhyming in Current Poetry

We often encounter assonant rhyming in day-to-day language (e.g., in phrases like "mean streets," "shoot hoops," and "live wire"), and it is ubiquitous in popular music (a random example being lines from a Neil Young song, "I have a friend I've never seen./ He hides his head inside a dream . . ."). In poetry, by contrast, assonant end-rhyme has a long history of being viewed as a telltale sign of a poet's lack of skill. To better grasp this reputation's apparent rehabilitation, it will be helpful briefly to look backward in time to gain some historical perspective of disapproval and stirrings in the direction of acceptance of such assonant end-rhymes as *husk/ dust, call/ waft,* and *swept/ depths.*

In 1936, *The Complete Rhyming Dictionary and Poet's Craft Book* was published, an updated edition of which remains in print. While this dictionary may read quaintly and often amusingly today, it portrays something of the taste and sentiment of its time. Furthermore, despite the dictionary's often dated stances, various of its ideals continue to survive in assorted states of health and decline.

In the dictionary's introduction, the editor, Clement Wood, briefly examines the ABCs of prosody, factually describing the various meters and stanzaic forms. In the midst of these workmanly passages appears a section entitled "Correct and Incorrect Rhyme." In this section, Wood begins, "Rhyme is as simple to define as rhythm is difficult," and goes on confidently to note that the only "correct" rhymes are of the variety of *ate/ bait/ plate/ mate/ abate/ straight/ syncopate.*

From the perspective of our allegedly kinder, gentler, politically correct age (the social workers of which eschew "labeling language"), we might find amusement in Wood's confident zest in making his rounds, segregating the good poets from the bad: "Slovenly rhyming is one of the sure signs of mediocrity in versification." Wood provides several examples of "slovenly" rhymes, including *real/ steal* and *childhood/ wildwood.* On the subject of the in-

26

advisability of attempting to rhyme *north* with *forth*, Wood notes, "If the poet is tone deaf as to sounds, it is best to rely upon the phonetic symbols above each group of the rhyming words in this book."

Wood singles out both consonance and assonance as "incorrect rhyme." In the case of the former, he notes the unacceptability of such consonant slant rhyme (or "sour rhyme") as *earth/hearth* and *silver/deliver*. However, even as Wood was pontificating on the slovenliness of consonant slant rhyme-endings, Yeats and Hopkins were in the midst of writing the poems which brought about their acceptance in British and American poetry.

The idea of using consonant slant-rhyme line-endings had not sprung into these poets' heads *ex nihilo*. Rather, the ground had been broken with earlier poets' efforts. In the seventeenth century, Henry Vaughan was one of the earliest English poets to attempt to incorporate consonant slant rhymes as end-rhymes. Later in America, Emerson and Dickinson vigorously embraced consonant slant-rhyme line-endings, though their efforts generally continued to be viewed as more or less odd until the wide acceptance of Yeats' and Hopkins' poetry. Since the canonization of Yeats' and Hopkins' poetry, con-sonant slant-rhyme line-ending has attained general acceptability, even among the most archly judgmental of formalist poets and readers.

Thus, at the twentieth century's beginning, rhymed poetry had two step-children: consonance and assonance. The two were identical twins insofar as the low opinion afforded them as instruments of end-rhyme. Both were relegated to the status of "translator's rhymes." During the Modernist period, one of these twins was adopted into legitimacy, while assonance continued to languish in disrepute. However, even Clement Wood, from his 1930s perspec-tive of prosodic purity noted, "Unpopular so far, at any time assonance may achieve a popularity in English versification."

Indeed, just as Vaughan and others had laid the preliminary groundwork for greater acceptance of consonant end-rhyme, some degree of ground-work had been laid for the emergence of assonant end-rhyme. For example, George Eliot made early attempts in this direction, as in the following excerpt with its assonant end-rhymes of *blackness/dances* and *roaming/floating*:

> Maiden, crowned with glossy blackness,
> Lithe as panther forest-roaming,
> Long-armed naead, when she dances,
> On the stream of ether floating . . .
>
> (*The Spanish Gypsy*)

While Emily Dickinson is recognized as one of the pioneers in legitimizing consonant slant-rhyme line-endings, it should also be noted that she often relied upon assonant end-rhymes as a means of infusing her poetry with further variety, liveliness and unpredictability. Assonant line-endings were tools for many of her most haunting prosodic effects. Assonant end-rhyme is present in one version of her portrayal of Death as a gentleman caller. When we recall the degree to which readers of her day were unaccustomed to assonant end-rhymes, those readers would have heard her long *a*-sounds (*played/grain*) as intoning a dream-like, almost senile imbalance:

> We passed the school where children played,
> Their lessons scarcely done—
> We passed the fields of gazing grain—
> We passed the setting sun—

A consonant sound tends to be stronger and more assertive than vowel sounds; hence, the weaker assonant end-rhyme in the above excerpt sounds the note of human fragility and evanescence, within Dickinson's often-visited context of eternity. In *The Poem's Heartbeat*, Alfred Corn describes Dickinson's use of assonant line-endings as providing some of her poems with a dissonant quality: "The incomplete, assonantal rhymes might be read as reinforcing a sense of mismatch, of separation from divine assurances . . . the assonantal rhymes appeal to the ear as part of the poem's dissonant texture."

Dickinson also employed distant assonance (*awe/fair, bed/break*) to instill a sense of breathy sacredness and reverential hush in the following well-known passage:

> Ample make this bed—
> Make this bed with awe—
> In it wait till Judgment break
> Excellent and fair. . . .

Consonance and alliteration often *bounce* the reader to a surface, rather than the reader *sinking into* the poem's sound, e.g., Vachel Lindsay's, "Booth led boldly with his big, bass drum." By contrast, Dickinson's stanza lacks the neat consonant click of closure. She uses vowel sounds quietly to infuse vocalic recessiveness, their inexactness harkening back to the preverbal and to the moan that emerges from dream-sleep.

Fast-forwarding in time, we encounter assonant end-rhyme mutating into modernity in the poetry of Dylan Thomas, as in his "Poem in October." Crisp Modernist Matisse-like visual color softens in the following passage, losing its edges and boundaries in sound (*stone/flows, blue/tune*), achieving an aural dimension divergent from Matisse's delineated boundaries:

> Over the blue stone
> Blue water flows,
> And clouds in the blue
> Silence of the deep tune.

Around the same time in America, assonant rhyme was an interest of Weldon Kees, a poet who has been much admired by and who has influenced several of our time's formalist poets. The following is an example of Kees' use of assonant line-ending. The passage provides an example of a lyric poise which has influenced passages in Dana Gioia's poetry:

> And shores and strands and naked piers,
> Sunset on waves, orange laddering the blue,
> White sails on headlands, cool
> Wide curving bay, dim landward distances
> Dissolving in the property of local air.

> ("Henry James at Newport")

Here Kees uses the assonant line-ending of *blue/cool*, among other devices, to produce the effect of fresh, seaside expansiveness and easiness. The partnering of the soothing *u*-sounds of *blue* and *cool* accentuates the seaside's physical sensation of happy release. Incidentally, this passage is interesting to examine in noting how easily Kees could have modified this stanza to attain a more conventional rhyme, simply by dropping the *s* from *piers* which then would have become a consonant slant rhyme with *air*. However, beyond the question of accurately portraying the landscape, Kees favored leaving the *s* on *piers*, preferring for it to echo the *s* on *distances*; thus, *piers* and *distances* become sonically linked in the reader's ear, subtly joining in the reader's mind to accentuate the described beach's and seaside's open distances. Also the resultant sonic separation of *piers/air* produces a gracefully indefinite closure at the stanza's end, the word *air* somewhat but not really rhyming with the distantly preceding *pier*, Kees allowing *air*'s heavy, diffusive vowel sound to hang at stanza's end.

29

Current formalist poetry ranges into degrees of variation in all aspects of its prosody, from rhyme to meter to the structures of given forms. Before focusing on current uses of assonance, we might first gain an insight into this general climate of variation. A quick means of doing so is to note some activity surrounding the sonnet. With exasperation in the *Hudson Review*, Robert Phillips discussed the anthology *Rebel Angels: 25 Poets of the New Formalism*:

> The inclusion of the Leithauser bastard form is but one of a number of [the anthology's] editorial mistakes or lapses in judgment. Others include Julia Alvarez's "hybrid sonnets" with deviant rhymes (live/psychoanalyzed). Mary Jo Salter's 9-line poem is called a "curtal sonnet," as is Wyatt Prunty's 8-line "Insomnia." At least Prunty's reads like an octave in search of a sestet. Molly Peacock's "The Wheel" is presented as a "Double Sonnet," yet consists of 29 lines, not 28. Peacock's English sonnet, "Desire," is highly irregular in meter. Another poem is called an "Exploded Sonnet," because it runs to 16 lines. Does this mean we can look forward to Exploded Haiku?

Phillips' wry comments provide a context for examining the current use of assonant end-rhyme among formalist poets. Phillips judges that, in many cases, more zeal than care is being applied to the production of sonnets. By extension, we may infer the same is likely true with rhyming. In other instances, avoidance of rhyme's exactitude comfortably and appropriately fits with the turn of the millennium, when neat rhymes might seem largely out of step with life's less neat actualities.

Though the Yeats of Assonance has yet to emerge, assonant end-rhyme is currently attracting many poets' impulses, to the degree that use of assonant end-rhyme would be more accurately described as *commonplace* than *experimental*; the word *experimental* implies a conscious decision to break with convention, while most of today's assonant end-rhymes seem simply the products of poets' natural inclinations. American formalist poets appear to be using assonant end-rhyme as a tool for achieving a wide range of poetic effects. In other cases, poets simply are feeling increasingly comfortable in substituting an assonant end-rhyme when an attractive exact rhyme seems unavailable, much as earlier became acceptable practice with consonant slant rhyme.

In presenting the following excerpts, I do not suggest that these poets have a conscious agenda of systematically incorporating assonant end-rhymes into their poetry. However, the following examples indicate poets' increasing comfort with employing occasional or, in the cases of some poets, frequent assonant rhyme-endings, certainly more so than would have been the case in earlier phases of American formalist poetry.

The following lines are excerpted from Alfred Corn's quasi-villanelle, "Shores" *(The Various Light)*. The lines' assonant endings *(distant/back, seed/between)* contribute to the poem's inwardly attentive lyric poise:

> These seeded grasses, stirred by a distant
> Earthquake, nod indicative heads to call back
> What I was. And am I alone here? Silent . . .
> . . . A stem flexes between root and seed.
> I feel the elation, the torsion between
> What I was and am. I, alone here, silent . . .

The following lines are excerpted from Henry Taylor's sonnet, "One Morning, Shoeing Horses" *(The Flying Change)*. The assonant *hoof/move* line-endings soften and relax the homely portrayal of a man coaxing a horse to relax to be shoed. Here I am reminded of Alfred Corn's comment in *The Poem's Heartbeat* that "a glancing quality, a leaner sound than full rhyme" provides a particular pleasure associated with a "sparer aesthetic":

> . . . touching his neck, turning his head to coax
> a little weight away from the lifted hoof,
> the flywhisk light and always on the move,
> the soothing whispers tuned to hammer strokes . . .

In a recent issue of *Sparrow*, Jared Carter uses assonant rhyme-ending *(path/half)* in the opening quatrain of his poem about Emily Dickinson ("Visit"). The word *half* beautifully does double sonic duty, with 1) its assonant partnering with *path* and 2) the *l* in *half* also echoing *falling/calling*. This sophisticated sonic interaction evokes a tone of quiet ghostliness:

> Whatever day you choose, rain will be falling
> out of the granite sky. Whatever path
> you take will make no sound. A lone bird calling
> through the double row of hemlocks seems half
> silenced by the gathering mist . . .

Charles Martin amusingly ventures into the vocalic in "Leaving Buffalo" *(Room for Error)*. In this poem of Italian quatrains in tight, traditional rhymes,

Martin suddenly veers into a sonically complicated partnering of *manners/ savannas*, the two words blending both assonant and consonant echoes of one another. Thus, the stanza ends with a heavy, longing vowel-sigh of *savanna's a-* sound (a sigh for the "apple-breasted women"?), a softer note as compared to the poem's otherwise metronomic regularity of perfect rhymes:

> ". . . When what will last of us are our manners?"
> They called abhorrent what was merely lewd,
> But dreamt of apple-breasted women: nude,
> Bronze-skinned lovelies of the far savannas. . . .

In the following excerpt from "The End of the Season" (*Daily Horoscope*), Dana Gioia uses assonant line-endings (*lake/away, clear/streets*) to create a softening, quieting effect. The stanza's only perfect rhyme-pairing is *tonight/ starlight*, which frames the stanza, the rhyme of this pair being greatly muted and softened by being separated by four intervening lines, this separation producing a delicate lyric echo. Internal rhymes and assonance enhance quiet musicality. The reader might notice resemblances between the use of this excerpt's assonance and general style and the earlier-discussed passage from Weldon Kees, indicating Kees' influence on Gioia:

> I wanted to tell you how I walked tonight
> down the hillside to the lake
> after the storm had blown away
> and say how everything suddenly seemed so clear
> against the sparkling, rain-soaked streets
> cold and bright as starlight.

Molly Peacock often is free in positioning rhymes in varying stanzaic positions within single poems, combining assonant end-rhymes with slant consonant end-rhymes and perfect rhymes. In fact, Peacock goes further than relying on assonant rhymes, often choosing imperfect assonance, as the following excerpts demonstrate. This fluidity of types and positions of rhymes combines with chattiness of tone, resulting in a texture which might be described as verse longing to be prose. Her poem "Painted Desert" (*Take Heart*) is for the most part traditionally rhymed throughout, though the opening quatrain uses the imperfect assonant pairing of *most/wolf*, which sets a normative rhyme for the poem that is less literary than might be the case if all four lines were tightly rhymed:

Connivers are the victims I hate most,
feeling close to them in mindset. Take this
Navaho below this sign, "See Live Pet Wolf."
Oh, the wolf is there all right, chained, while his . . .

In "Say You Love Me" (*Take Heart*), Peacock writes tercets in which perfect rhymes, consonant slant rhymes and assonant end-rhymes all swirl, mirroring the confusion of the poem's tempestuous situation in which the poet as a girl is portrayed being emotionally abused by her father. Assonant end-rhyme abounds, playing off of perfect rhymes: *of/was/above, because/jaws/love, me/fifteen/she, been/mean/knee, age/gazed*. Peacock attempts to strike a tonal balance between realistic description which is almost journalistic and a sound distantly reminiscent of the balladic. The imperfect assonant end-rhymes help the poem remain closer to earthy realism than might be the case if the narrative were accented more consistently with perfect rhymes:

> . . . by defeat into a cardboard image, untrue,
> unbending. I was surprised I could move
> as I did to get up, but he stayed, burled . . .

In *Whirling Round the Sun*, Suzanne Noguere occasionally turns to assonant end-rhyme to loosen up passages into humor, as in her sonnet entitled "My Grandmother Nellie Braun." In this sonnet, the first perfectly rhymed Sicilian quatrain (*fall/deck/tall/neck*) presents factual description of the grandmother. The second quatrain's rhyme scheme reinforces the poem's departure into humor; its two rhyme-partners veer into variance, with assonant end-rhyme (*flaws/calls*) as well as a whimsical slant rhyme (*coarse as/horses*):

> . . . length hair, cut blunt and snooded, became as coarse as
> sailmakers' thread. Bright eyes belied all flaws:
> "I don't drink, gamble, or play the horses,"
> she said, explaining the long distance calls.

With the first poem in Noguere's collection ("Ear Training for Poets"), we encounter, ". . . a melody where April and maple meld," and recognize a poet with a pleasure-taking attentiveness to language's sounds. The structure of her poem, "Robert Johnson," about the blues musician, includes positions for seven rhyme partners, which she fills with five perfect end-rhymes and two assonant end-rhymes (*coax/ghost* and *last/epitaph*). This latter coupling is especially creative in its rhyme:

> . . . the heart that always goes for broke can't last
> longer than to write its fast epitaph.

As this essay has emphasized, there has been a long history of viewing assonant end-rhyme as a mediocre poet's clumsy default in lieu of perfect rhyme or consonant rhyme. Within such a context, Noguere's quoted passage almost appears to be throwing down the gauntlet in behalf of assonance. In her clever sonic construction of *can't last/fast epitaph*, she overtly subordinates perfect end-rhyme in favor of assonant end-rhyme. In this couplet, the two end-rhymes are assonant (*last/epitaph*), while the first of the two partners (*last*) is a perfect rhyme for *fast*, the word preceding (and, hence, being subordinated to) the end-rhyme proper. As a further introduction of vocalic music, Noguere places the assonant echo *can't* just before the first of the two rhyme-partners. This couplet is a sign of our times in terms of formal poetry's increasing comfort with and even preference for assonance.

In his translator's note to the *Inferno*, Robert Pinsky describes his translation's system of consonant slant rhyme: "This system of like sounds happens to respond to some preference of my own ear, a personal taste: for me such rhymes as, say, 'swans/stones' or 'gibe/club' or 'south/both' often sound more beautiful and interesting than such hard-rhyme combinations as 'bones/stones,' 'rub/club,' or 'south/mouth.' " Thus, Pinsky emphasizes his contemporary unease with what can sometimes feel like the blatancy of perfect rhyme; as a solution to his wanting to adapt Dante's terza rima for current poetry, he relies on the consonant slant rhyme which he describes as being of his personal taste, also acknowledging an adherence to precedents set by Yeats. Rather than consonant slant rhyme being the "preference of [Pinsky's] own ear", it is probably the case that his ear has been conditioned by the work of poets who preceded him in the previous century, while current trends certainly are conditioning "personal preference . . . personal taste" to assonant end-rhyme.

Kevin Durkin

Far from Pedestrian

The checkered sneakers stolen from a child
and yoked together with a knot of laces
now hang suspended from a power line,
transcending hopscotch, tetherball, and races.

Until a lineman comes to cut them down,
the pair will slowly twist as nature pleases,
darkened by rain or fading in the sun,
their soles tap-dancing in the lightest breezes.

John Beaton

Lost Overnight in the Woods

The horizon garrottes the twilight's throat. I sleep-walk
through slash and over deadfall. My arms, white canes,
antenna me through copses; touching tree-trunks,
legs of huge tenebrios, whose abdomens
are canopies of darkness under elytra,
I walk. Winds whisper mantra after mantra.

Now branches frieze the sky—wrought-iron frost-work
Sistines the darkling beetles' undersides.
I see an Agincourt arrow, a kingfisher, flash-track,
grey, but fletched with blurs of blues and reds,
through ribs of fallen trees that cage a reach
where swans' necks question whether day will break.

A bull-elk rears. His forelegs scissor the moon-rays.
He splashes down, legs thrashing the water, then dips
his head in the glister, raises his rack like a sunrise,
shakes it, smithereening his crown, then grasps
the horizon's rope in his antlers; with a swing and a sling,
throws bolas at darkness's legs and unstrangles the sun.

John Beaton

Heat in the Blood

Your festival stirs it, Saint Fermin. You bishoped Pamplona's see
till they severed your head and its sermons, the head that Saint Saturnine wetted
at the baptismal font in Toulouse. He was towed to his martyry
on a rope by a running bull. Now the cobbles are castanetted

by the beating of taurine hooves. The corral has its gates flung wide
and the bull-pack are surging like galleons as they forge through this flesh-and-blood strait
where, from fervor to fear, then to frenzy, the runners careen, saucer-eyed
as the Curva de Mercaderes makes a flume for the human spate.

They commit to what Hemingway wrote of so bravely but never once dared:
to tie on a scarlet bandana, drink wine, and, breakneck, to run
on the horns at the tips of the prongs, then to swerve for the throng and be spared
the *cornada*, the wound that would snuff out their Also-Rising Sun.

The bulls now explode through the Plaza, where, long before dusk, they will thrust,
pagan, against the *estoque*. And their blood will then steam from your dust.

Dick Davis

Translations from the Persian

for Turner and Suzanne

If that full moon were true and good,
                    how would that be?
And if he feared God as he should,
                    how would that be?

I'd like to stay with him a while—
If he decided that I could,
                    how would that be?

I long to kiss his lovely lips,
And if he said he thought I should,
                    how would that be?

And if that idol I pursue
Pursued me too, and understood,
                    how would that be?

Or if one day that king should glance
At where this helpless beggar stood,
                    how would that be?

If wisdom followed me around,
Or if I'd sense and hardihood,
                    how would that be?

If happiness should lead Obayd
To him, supposing that it could,
                    how would that be?

Obayd-e Zakani (14th century)

★ ★

Well once upon a time, in dribs and drabs,
Income turned up for me, throughout the year;

I'd dry bread and fresh herbs to hand, in case
A friend should unexpectedly appear;

And sometimes there'd be wine to drink, for when
A pretty boy or sweet young girl came here.

But now I'm getting on in years my life
Has suddenly become much more austere;

I've neither dry to eat, nor wet to drink,
And all that's in my house is me, my dear.

Obayd-e Zakani

★ ★

Last night, my love, my life, you lay with me,
I grasped your pretty chin, I fondled it,
And then I bit, and bit, your sweet lips till
I woke . . . It was my fingertip I bit.

Princess Jahan Khatun (14th century)

★ ★

My friend, who was so kind and faithful once,
Has changed his mind now, and I don't know why;

I think it must be in my wretched stars—
He feels no pity for me when I cry.

Oh I complain of your cruel absence, but
Your coming here's like dawn's breeze in the sky;

That oath you swore to and then broke—thank God
It's you who swore, and is foresworn, not I!

I didn't snatch one jot of joy before
You snatched your clothes from me and said goodbye;

I didn't thank you, since I wasn't sure
You'd really been with me, or just passed by.

How envious our clothes were when we lay
Without them, clasped together, you and I!

Your curls have chained my heart up; this is right—
Madmen are chained up, as they rage and sigh.

They say the world's lord cherishes his slaves;
So why's he harsh to me? I don't know why.

Princess Jahan Khatun (14th century)

The Sultan's Crown

A brief second spent grieving her loss is worth more than all the world.
Sell your sufi-robe for wine, it's good for nothing else.

The wine-dealers won't do business; whatever I have,
the prayer-mat of my stern devotions . . . isn't worth a cup.

The gate-keeper turned me away; what's happened
that I'm not worth the dust on your doorstep?

The sultan's crown holds the power of life and death—
it's attractive, sure, but not worth risking your head.

How easy it seemed at first, sailing the flood in quest of treasure . . .
Now, I wouldn't leave shore for a thousand pearls.

Better you should hide your face from your lovers,
the joy of victory's not worth the trouble of keeping captives.

In free surrender, struggle on like Hafiz, forgetting the world . . .
even if the least seed of effort should repay your weight in gold.

— *Translated from the Persian of Hafiz*
  by Jeffrey Einboden and John Slater

Kevin Durkin

An Interview with Timothy Steele

I first heard Timothy Steele read in the most unlikely of places—at Beyond Baroque, a bookstore cum arts center in Venice, California. I say unlikely because although Steele, a native Vermonter, has lived in the Los Angeles area for more than two decades, he is not the sort of poet one usually associates with that particular venue, where the spirit of the late Charles Bukowski still holds some sway.

The night of the reading, which Steele shared with fellow metrical poet Leslie Monsour, who studied with Steele in the late 1980s and who is herself now emerging as a strong new voice in American poetry, was a particularly inauspicious one: the hardest rain of the season descended just prior to Monsour and Steele's scheduled hour, and since Angelenos tend to think of rain the way people on the Mid-Atlantic Coast think of snow, only fifteen or so people had ventured onto the freeways to come hear them read. Clad in a black turtleneck and tweed jacket, Steele looked every inch the English professor that he is, but rather than assume a studied role for the occasion, he simply read his poems and commented between them with casual good humor. The small audience was clearly a discerning and appreciative one, and the reading was one of the best I have ever attended.

Although I had vaguely heard of Steele before I moved to the Los Angeles area in 1996, I had not read his verse until the month before his Beyond Baroque reading, and I was still reeling from the experience. He writes witty and elegant metrical poems that frequently employ perfect rhymes, something you seldom encounter in poetry these days. Never having met a free verse poem I would willingly commit to memory, and long an admirer of Robinson, Frost, Larkin, and Wilbur, I'd begun to think that there was no one of a younger generation than Wilbur's who possessed the talent for, and commitment to, metrical poetry that I so eagerly sought.

Yes, I had read most of the New Formalists, but much of their poetry struck me as lacking three essential ingredients: sensuous appeal, crackling wit, and colorful imagination. Steele's poetry—although often lumped together with that of other New Formalists—has all three of these ingredients in abundance. I recall with special pleasure a poem he read at Beyond Baroque about his neighborly exchanges with an elderly woman. Before reading the poem, Steele mentioned that it contained an allusion to Frost's "Mending Wall," a hint that made me prick up my ears. The allusion certainly wasn't hard to detect, but how cleverly it had been deployed.

Fae

I bring Fae flowers. When I cross the street,
She meets and gives me lemons from her tree.
As if competitors in a Grand Prix,
The cars that speed past threaten to defeat
The sharing of our gardens and our labors.
Their automotive moral seems to be
That hell-for-leather traffic makes good neighbors.

Ten years a widow, standing at her gate,
She speaks of friends, her cat's trip to the vet,
A grandchild's struggle with the alphabet.
I conversationally reciprocate
With talk of work at school, not deep, not meaty.
Before I leave we study and regret
Her alley's newest samples of graffiti.

Then back across with caution: to enjoy
Fae's lemons, it's essential I survive
Lemons that fellow Angelenos drive.
She's eighty-two; at forty, I'm a boy.
She waves goodbye to me with her bouquet.
This place was beanfields back in '35
When she moved with her husband to L.A.

I found myself laughing out loud at Steele's play on "lemons" in the third stanza, and then sobering up considerably for the poem's quietly moving conclusion. Re-reading this poem at home that night, I realized with pleasure that Steele had captured quite a lot about life in Los Angeles in just twenty-one flawless lines of verse.

"Fae" is one of many excellent poems that appeared in Steele's most recent collection, *The Color Wheel*, which was published in 1994 by Johns Hopkins

University Press. Extending the range and depth of his two previous books of poetry (available as a single volume, *Sapphics and Uncertainties,* from the University of Arkansas Press), *The Color Wheel* confidently establishes Steele not only as the premiere metrical poet of his generation but also as one of the very best poets writing in English today.

Steele is also an exceptional critic. His study of the modern revolt against meter, *Missing Measures,* met with more criticism than praise for exposing the misconceptions about meter that Pound and Eliot labored under—misconceptions that continue to haunt the art of poetry and have given rise not only to the ungainly free verse that overwhelms us today, but also to a growing tide of shoddy verse that passes for being metrical. Perceived by many as a threat to the status quo, *Missing Measures* has also been arousing clarion call to a younger generation of poets interested in the history and practice of their art. *Missing Measures* and Steele's own poetry are two of the most significant, if least acknowledged, reasons why metrical poetry has been making a comeback in American literary journals.

Steele's most recent book, *All the Fun's in How You Say a Thing: An Explanation of Meter and Versification,* appeared in 1999 from Ohio University Press, and although sales have been strong in the States and it has been recently reviewed at great length in the *Times Literary Supplement,* it has yet to receive a review in a major American publication. This is a grave oversight, because the book is quite simply the most comprehensive, accurate, and enjoyable book of its kind.

Since I first heard Steele read at Beyond Baroque a few years ago, I have met with him on several occasions and have exchanged e-mails with him weekly. The following interview was conducted mostly by e-mail during the early months of the year 2000—the perfect time, we both felt, to discuss Steele's most recent book and the state of the art of poetry at the dawn of the new millennium.

KD: Tim, let's start with the new book. What prompted you to write *All the Fun's in How You Say a Thing?*

TS: There are several answers to that. One is that I've always loved metered verse and wanted to explain the advantages meter offers poets and the pleasures it gives readers.

KD: What sort of advantages do you mean?

TS: Against the bass line of the meter, a poet can register shades of rhythm and tone with special sensitivity. Also, poets can play the meter off against grammar. They can run sentence structure through the end of the metrical unit or, conversely, achieve extra emphasis by endstopping—by making metrical units and syntactical ones coincide. What's more, working in meter—and with the related devices of rhyme and stanza—you find the form forcing you to think of all sorts of alternative ways of phrasing thoughts and feelings. As you try to secure this or that cadence or rhyme, you start thinking of things that otherwise would not have occurred to you. In this sense, meter can be mentally and emotionally enlarging.

KD: Could you give an example of an experience of this sort that you had while writing one of your own poems?

TS: This happened with one of the first poems I wrote—"History of a Friendship in Mattapoisett." The poem's about how relationships work and don't work. When I was first trying to write the poem, I hadn't grasped its theme sufficiently. But at one point I needed an iambic tetrameter whose final syllable would rhyme with "unsaid"; and playing with phrases that fit the meter and words that met the rhyme, I came up with "Tact is at once acquired and shed." And it dawned on me that, yes, this was the point of the poem: as we get to know people better, we put aside conventional politesse, but at the same time we need to cultivate deeper forms of tact, remembering that other people are just that—other than we are—and we have to respect the difference, no matter how close we grow to them. Anyway, I don't think I'd have been able to clarify the poem, or have been able to understand the relationship that occasioned it, had it not been for the form. The meter and rhyme made me think harder and feel along different lines than I might have done normally.

KD: What other advantages are there to writing in meter?

TS: Well, metrical poetry is also just plain fun. Though it has rules, once you start working within their boundaries, you find all sorts of interesting challenges.

KD: You also mentioned the pleasure metrical poetry gives readers.

TS: Rhythmically organized verse is catchier—it's easier to remember—than free verse. Meter offers a sensuous appeal to the ear and mind. And

45

poetic form can in general create all sorts of pleasurable symmetries and surprises. A poem with formal structure can achieve a beauty and fullness that a poem without such structure can't. Structure gives a poem resistant grace and power. A fine metrical poem by Richard Wilbur, Janet Lewis, Louise Bogan, Philip Larkin, X. J. Kennedy, Edgar Bowers, Thom Gunn, or Anthony Hecht or—to go back a little further—a good sonnet by Robert Frost or Countee Cullen feels like it's built to last. And I think many readers are grateful for the poet's having taken the time to create something that has focus and comeliness.

KD: Do you think poets and critics have lost sight of these qualities?

TS: They have been, I fear, largely forgotten in the wake of modernism and the triumph of free verse. And in *All the Fun's in How You Say a Thing* I wanted to make available, for those who might be interested, a book that was accurate and helpful and that might stand as an alternative to the false things that are often said today about meter and its history.

KD: Could you give some examples of the sort of false things you mean?

TS: One very destructive notion—Pound and Eliot were responsible for it, though they didn't mean to harm poetry—is that regular meter and individual rhythm are mutually exclusive and that to write rhythmically interesting verse you have to break or violate the meter. A more general fallacy, it seems to me, is that form is a straitjacket and that regularity is inevitably inhibiting. In fact, form can be enabling in the same way that any structure can be. We couldn't move as well or as variously as we do if we didn't have a skeleton, and the metric frame, to use Frost's term, gives you all sorts of different possibilities for organizing speech. Another common fallacy is that meter is somehow elitist. Anyone who's listened to pop songs, which are almost always heavily metered, knows this isn't true. But a number of poets and critics, including one of our recent poet laureates, still regularly repeat this notion.

KD: It has always struck me as odd that something as neutral as meter has been so often criticized in this way. Some practitioners of free verse, such as Eliot and Pound, certainly had elitist tendencies. And some metrical poets—Robert Burns leaps to mind—clearly did not.

TS: It's strange how the history of free verse is lost on so many *vers-libristes*, especially those in the United States. The pioneers of free verse saw themselves as Nietzschean überpoets, revolting against petty bourgeois literary convention. And as you say, leading experimentalists like Pound and Eliot had views about politics and society that were pretty right-wing. Today, however, the ideas Pound and Eliot developed are often propounded by those who see free verse as egalitarian, on the dubious grounds that anybody can write it. I say "dubious" because there are all sorts of activities, including using firearms or driving recklessly, which pretty much anybody can engage in, but which are hardly egalitarian. If Pound and Eliot knew how their ideas are currently being employed, they'd probably be spinning in their graves. By the same token, many contemporary anti-metrists would likely be horrified if they knew where their arguments came from.

KD: Was there anything else that motivated you to write *All the Fun's in How You Say a Thing*? Surely your experience as a teacher of literature and poetry at Cal State Los Angeles must have played some role.

TS: As the late Henri Coulette once observed, meter seems to have become almost a lost language. And if you care about poetry and go into a college classroom and discover that no one knows what a sonnet or heroic couplet is, you start to wonder if you should try to do something about the situation. At least that's what eventually happened with me. There were some useful prosody books on the market—one being James McAuley's *Versification: A Short Introduction*. But even it seemed to suffer from the problem from which most of the standard digests or manuals suffer. In the interests of compression, the subject is presented in a clinically abrupt manner, with very few examples, and many interesting or important issues must be oversimplified or ignored. I didn't want to do this. I wanted to write a book that attempted to cover pretty much the full field. I hoped to write a book that would be thorough and fun to read, filled with lots of examples from good poets and shaped by the concerns of a practicing poet.

KD: I think readers will agree, Tim, that you've accomplished what you've set out to do.

TS: Thank you.[7]

---

[7] *To learn more about Timothy Steele and his work, visit his web site at http://curriculum.calstatela.edu/faculty/tsteele/.*

Stephen Edgar

The Music of What Happens

It is to this all art aspires,
They say,
When those twin helices, the double gyres
Of form and content turn as one instead,
Until whatever sense they may
Be said to have, though sensed, cannot be said.

And isn't that what happens here
From day
To day, this fashioning they engineer
Of time through time: the way the air arranges
The sky or makes the treetops sway,
Or washing wrestles with its shadow changes;

A thermal rises from the plain;
A wave
Crawls emptily and lets the sea remain;
An intricately moulded sheet of water,
Flung from a plastic pail to lave
The pavement by a neighbour's squealing daughter,

Casts a transparent, dimpled, belled,
Ruched, laced
And pleated arc, which almost seems upheld
Against its own liquidity and weight,
Then breaks, its shattered wetness traced
Like shadows, though they soon evaporate.

Stephen Edgar

Cinematic History

With leer to camera, flourishing his cape,
And twirling fingers at his waxed moustache,
The villain pauses, and then makes his dash
Towards the damsel with her mouth agape.

The screen blacks out a moment for suspense
And in the gap the words "She screams" replace
The awful action. Then that gaping face.
But the only screams are from the audience.

Silence and overacting. Hard to believe
That those who watched it new could then evince
Real fear, real pity, while you simply wince
And wipe your tears of laughter with a sleeve.

So cinema. And so the present tense,
If you could make your focus slow enough,
Like those exploding windows full of stuff
That end *Zabriskie Point*, in an immense

And multifarious pageant past your eyes,
Would slide from the invisible display
Of naked custom that you wear today
Without a second thought, into the guise

Of dated costume drama, first suspicious,
Then ever more outlandish and extreme,
And hardly thinkable. Its figures seem
Bad actors, and their heartfelt truths fictitious,

Until suspension fails your disbelief.
How could you bear the accumulated weight
If all the players did not dissipate
To fancy, lost to life, then death, and grief?

49

Freeway

Mary Anne and Jackson were lost in that part of Miami that tourists only know about from their TV sets. "Jesus Christ," Jackson said. "I should've known you couldn't manage this. All you had to do was get us from the fucking airport to your Aunt's house." He looked over at her from behind the wheel, smiling in the way that said she was lucky he was being so patient. "But that was too much for my little Mary Anne, wasn't it?" He shook his head, wagging it from side to side. "Wasn't it, honey?"

Mary Anne clenched her fists around the corners of the map and looked back at her husband.

"Careful honey," he said, pointing to the map. "You don't want to ruin that. It's your only shot at getting us out of this."

Mary Anne was silent for a minute, then she said, "What would you like me to do?"

"What I would like you to do," Jackson said, "Is to function like a halfway intelligent human being." He turned toward her again. "Just for *once*. You think you can do that?"

"Sure," said Mary Anne.

They were driving down streets that seemed to get more narrow and rutted the farther they went. She looked out the window at the long, aquamarine and pink warehouses on the side of the road, at the heavy, ponderous sky, at the palm trees that seemed ready to catch whatever it decided to unleash. Everywhere, in the corners of her frame of vision, there was movement. Small, scurrying, secretive movement. She felt it in her body, like something soft and electrifying running up and down her arms. We're being watched, she thought. This is bad. But she didn't feel anything in connection with the thought. It was just knowledge, it just *was*.

"Jesus fucking Christ," Jackson said. "Can you get us back to the freeway?" He gestured ahead of them, almost hitting the windshield. "It's right there, Mary Anne. Come *on*."

But they weren't getting back to the freeway. On and off-ramps loomed overhead, a curling mess of concrete and asphalt. They had been trying for at least a half hour to get to the on-ramp, and it wasn't happening. Mary Anne looked down at the map. It was a blur of red, green and black lines, twisting together beside the great blue expanse of the Atlantic Ocean. "I can't tell exactly where we are," she muttered. "Somewhere around here I think." She pointed vaguely at a section of small black lines that bordered the water.

Jackson grabbed the map, crumpled it in his fist, and threw it out the window. He turned to Mary Anne.

"What a disappointment you are, you stupid, stupid cunt. I never should have married you." He sighed and shook his head as if the inconvenience were too much for him.

"I'm sorry," Mary Anne said.

"I know you are," Jackson said. "That's why you're going to get out now and find us some nice gentleman who can give us directions."

Mary Anne looked out the window. They were stopped now, and the movement that had previously existed in the fringes of her field of vision seemed to be moving to the center. She saw a pair of arms and legs scuttle from behind one warehouse to the next. And another, behind a large brown dumpster that stood next to it.

Suddenly, seemingly out of nowhere, there was a knock on Jackson's window. "Yo man, you lost, eh? Your car broke?" He was grinning and had gleaming white and gold teeth.

Jackson rolled down the window. "We need to get to the freeway," he said.

"Yah, man, I understan." He pointed to the car. "Too bad your car broke, eh?"

"My car isn't broken—" Jackson started, but didn't finish. The man's hand reached in and grabbed Jackson around the neck. "I'm Julio!" he said, and then he pointed behind him, where three other men were standing, hands in their loose jean pockets. They wore sleeveless white tee-shirts which showed off their smooth brown arms.

"We gonna help you fix your car," he said, and before Mary Anne could stop to wonder how she felt about anything at all, Jackson had disappeared out the window. Mary Anne heard a soft thump as he hit the dirt.

Julio stared at her through the driver's side window. "Well, chica," he said. "You wan' me to help you fix your car?"

Mary Anne looked around for a minute, as if she had all the time in the world. There was no hurry. Somehow she knew that. The pale blue interior of their BMW 540i was littered with Jackson's cigarette butts, stuffed into the ashtray, and the bags of Sun Chips and M&Ms that she had bought at the convenience store where they stopped for gas. The motor was still running, and the air conditioner blasted cold air from the vents. Jackson Brown's "The Day the Music Died" played faintly from the speakers.

Julio waited patiently. Mary Anne looked at his face and in the gray afternoon light it looked somehow kind. The car was *in here*. The row of warehouses, of men with guns, probably, and packets of cocaine, god-knows-what-else were *out there*. Along with the water, and a freeway somewhere nearby, and her Aunt's house somewhere not far after that.

"If I give you this car," Mary Anne said, "Will you let me go?"

"Oh, honey . . ." Julio said. "You and your man here are gonna have to stay while we fix it." He grinned. "It's only fair," he said.

"No." Mary Anne opened the passenger door and got out of the car. She walked around to face Julio and saw that Jackson was lying on his stomach, face pressed into the dirt, grunting. One of the men sat on top of him and held his arms.

"Honey," he said pitifully. He seemed suddenly smaller than his 6 feet 4 inches.

"No," Mary Anne said again, and took a deep breath of wild, salty air. Everything was very clear.

"I'll give you the car," she said. "It'll make you good money on parts." She smiled. "You can have it." She turned around, looked in the direction of the freeway, and then turned back to Julio. "And you can have my husband, too."

Jackson made a strangled sound against the dirt.

"And you can have my credit cards—they're all in his name—and you can have my purse. It's a Prada. It's worth at least $350 now. And you can have my leather jacket—it's in the trunk—and my rings—" She wrenched them rapidly off her fingers. "I'm just keeping 20 bucks, boys, ok?" She rummaged in her purse, pulled out a twenty, then dumped the contents of her purse onto the dirt. While she did all of this, Mary Anne watched herself with a kind of stunned amusement, as if she were not, in point of fact, the person doing any of these things.

"I'm going, boys," she said. "Right now."

Julio hesitated, but she held up one finger. "This is a good deal and you know it," she said. "Now: which way to the freeway?"

Julio pointed to the left—the way they had never tried.

Annie Finch

Mowing

Easing the land into one long-plotted scene,
we stroke grass into piles with the rake.
Earth's face goes quiet, moved to a docile green
tinge blushed for other eyes, not for our sake.
Harrow the lawn, pack leaves of grass to loam,
flatten the seed-tall walls that would twist and sigh
around us, carve down the rooted caves that foam
with causeless silence, kill the lace-long sky.
Why harvest a grain whose worth is to remain
and ignore the seeds, leaving the yield unkept,
trudging lost kernels to such empty gain?
Won't we have reaped until we've stopped and swept
all the harvest away? Must we stand to see
our plain land lie with hands open, and empty?

Henna

I will call her Ms. Shari, even though she was married. Still, Ms. Shari is how the head of the department and I spoke of her in a tense, unhappy discussion behind closed doors.

I was teaching at a state university—crowded, underfunded, with clocks that never worked, irritable faculty and windowless rooms that induced fugue states. Still, it was generous, because it admitted almost everyone: The campus looked like an international mall. There were women in tight jeans and four inch heels, men with beards and turbans, mothers in saris wheeling babies, teenagers in yarmulkes, people in business suits who were ready to tell you they had degrees in physics, anthropology or phonetics but were getting an MBA to "shore things up." The elevators looked as though a sample population on a Manhattan subway had been transported. The school was a strange, cloned miracle: New York had merged with California.

The student in question was a woman who'd enrolled in a course I was teaching called Writing from Life. Her name was Ms. Shari. She sat alone in the back row next to the door, looking at her thick shoes, smoothing her chador, or touching her wrists. They were crowded with orange and green flowers as though the henna dots on her fingers had sprouted a garden. My students could write about anything—grocery lists, lovemaking, children, changing tires. Everybody wrote voluminously except for Ms. Shari who said her culture didn't believe in revealing anything personal and nothing she wrote could be less than that. When I asked why she'd taken the class she said she needed credits in English. Then she said: "What do you think? Should a life be open to the public?" Before I could answer she left. From then on she came to class every third meeting.

"Don't take that kind of thing," said Nicole, the department secretary. "Tell her to drop because she's flunking." Nicole, who wore large shaded glasses and designer suits, ran the English department. She knew the curriculum and figured out whose turn it was to teach freshman comp. She decided who should share offices. Nicole had given me a cherished key to the Xerox machine and made sure I never taught eight o'clocks so I could drive my fifteen-year-old to school. I wondered if telling Ms. Shari to drop the course was extreme. "Extreme?" said Nicole. "No one takes shit like that."

The next time Ms. Shari was in class, I leaned by her desk and told her she should drop the class because she was flunking. The cloth of her chador exuded a faint aroma of spice, reminding me of weather and sky I'd never seen. She picked up her books and left.

That day we talked about Sylvia Plath's journals. Most people thought they were a microcosmic view of an unhappy, roiling life. Some worried that writing about that life reified the pain and was responsible for Sylvia Plath's suicide. But Gabriel Gonzalez pointed out that Virginia Woolf's journals were macrocosmic sweeps of an outer world, and she'd committed suicide too. "So it might not matter how you wrote about your life," he said, "or even if you wrote at all." Gabriel was twenty-two and his eyes were failing: to focus, he used a rolled-up newspaper. It looked like a spyglass, confirming my impression that the windowless room was a ship and we were all in a hold underwater.

"Actually," said Miss Tapali, who was from the Philippines, "if you're already crazy, a journal won't make you crazier."

Everyone laughed except Gabriel Gonzalez: he approached almost everything with melancholy. After the class he stuffed the newspaper in his pocket and said he didn't see a problem with being crazy. I said I agreed as long as you could manage the world.

I was about to tell Gabriel—not for the first time—that he should try to get his work published. He knew I would say this and left before I had the chance. All at once, I heard a noise and saw Ms. Shari and another woman looming in the florescence at the door. The other woman was so tall I thought she might be a man wearing a chador. I felt a boundless fear and moved past them to the hall.

"I am a representative," the taller woman said, "and we are accusing you of racism. You have asked Ms. Shari to write things that are against our beliefs. You leaned down to talk to her in a condescending way. You never were clear about the assignments."

"This school is for everybody," she continued. "You can't ask people to do things against their religions. You are a racist and an intolerant person." Her voice rose and the international throng began to look at us. I said I couldn't change the way I taught. The representative said they would take the case to the dean, or, worse, to the president. She made her orange and blue hands into fists and said I would have to pay for my lack of understanding. Ms. Shari raised her fists, too. Their twenty painted fingers became tiny people endowed with magic, malevolent powers.

Nicole's office was at the end of the hall. Through her open door she saw everything through her shaded glasses. When the women left, I went to her office and began to cry. I hadn't cried in school since kindergarten when I'd been sent back from the playground for walking across fresh tanbark. Nicole closed the door and gave me chocolates filled with brandy.

"They're just crazy, that's all," she said. "You're not a racist. I know about that." Of course she did. Nicole was black and raised in the South.

That night while I tried to sleep the women's fists morphed into fabulous artifacts, dangerous codes, puppets with frightening powers. One thing stayed the same: they wanted to hurt me.

Two days later the head of the English department called me to his office. When I passed Nicole she shook her head and said, "I'm sorry."

The head of the department, who came from a distinguished line of Asian scholars, looked at me sternly through rimless glasses. There had been a complaint about me, he said, a serious complaint, and it was ill advised of me to take Nicole's advice. Perhaps, he continued, I wasn't used to teaching. Perhaps, he said delicately, I was "the artistic type" and never had written a syllabus. I knew it would be umbrage to tell him I taught in graduate programs: instead I showed him the syllabus, which he looked at carefully. When he found nothing wrong, he got more upset.

"Then the issue is racism," he said, "and racism is serious. Ms. Shari says you're asking her to do something against her religion."

I said maybe I was, but she'd taken the course. I tried to focus on his bookcase—Semiotics Applied to Keats, Reader Response and Henry James.

"She can't flunk," he said. "She absolutely can't. We're here to give people degrees. Everybody is entitled to a degree." He explained what would be involved if this were taken to the dean, and then to the president: "A disgrace to all of us."

Again I felt a boundless fear. I offered to meet with Ms. Shari privately to find out what felt right for her. This was the humility the head of the department wanted to hear.

"Oh no," he said. "No one expects you to spend that kind of time with a student or change a course. I'm going to tell Ms. Shari she has to turn in the assignments you ask for." He stood up. The meeting was over.

The next day Ms. Shari came to class and sat in the back the way she always did. She began to hand in work. Her pieces were so precise they reminded me of mosaics but I never told her because I was afraid she'd say I was thinking about her culture in stereotypes.

Because I must keep her writing confidential, there's only one piece I can paint in broad strokes: it was about how Ms. Shari and her husband celebrated their wedding anniversary on an early spring evening. They came home from work, ate lamb stew on a red and golden cloth upon the floor. They opened presents from their families and then, because working overtime was essential, both went back to their jobs. "This is how we live our lives," Ms. Shari wrote. "It's very simple."

I was in the middle of an acrimonious divorce. The piece made me think about my almost-former husband—the gifts we'd gotten, the gifts we'd lost. The pages felt like a door to her house—prayer rug, pillows, lamb. For a moment I walked inside.

At the end of class people read their work aloud: Ms. Tapali about training to be a law enforcement officer, Gabriel Gonzalez about meeting himself at every second of his life—an infinite number of Gabriel Gonzalezes with anxiety about future ones or grudges against previous ones. Ms. Shari, the last to volunteer, wrote about visiting her country for a relative's wedding. She wouldn't read it aloud, but agreed to answer questions if she could sit in the back. Everyone was curious: "What about men and women being segregated during a wedding?" "If our whole life consisted of going to weddings," she said, "it wouldn't be worth being married!" People laughed and asked more questions: "Has your history been recorded?" "At least as well as yours."

Even Gabriel Gonzalez fixed upon Ms. Shari with his newspaper spyglass. When she finished talking people applauded. She left without picking up her papers. I gave her an A.

Later, much later, when the university and its twilit rooms became an underwater dream, I found Ms. Shari's piece about her anniversary. I'd put it unthinkingly in a cabinet with rubber bands and stamps. Once more the pages became a door: the lamb, the blessing, the opening of gifts, I'd never forgotten her work, although I'd forgotten all the others except the extraordinary writing of Gabriel Gonzalez. Was it because of the difficulties with Ms. Shari? My unhappiness about my divorce? Or was there an aura of intimacy to her writing that belied her reluctance to write in the first place? The word beloved rose inside my heart. It was the beloved of old walled cities, hanging gardens. I discarded it as a romantic notion.

It was winter when I found her piece. Rain was beating on the skylights of my study—steady, endless rain that's poured on wooden roofs in Japan and mud huts in India and passes again and again through this northwestern sky. It drummed on the glass above my head. I wondered whether Ms. Shari's country also had rain.

Yes, it did, an atlas said. Deep, steady rain, except not nearly as frequent as rain in California. I remembered Ms. Shari's hands and wondered what it would be like to have my own hands decorated with henna. Was this a whim from a catalogue dreamt by a liquid metal bracelet by Sergio? Or did I want my hands to look like Ms. Shari's? I discarded the idea as another misplaced notion.

And then I forgot about Ms. Shari, until the World Trade Center shattered and everything about her became vivid. I remembered her sarcastic wit, her dark eyes, her thick shoes. I re-read everything she wrote and was obsessed with the idea that I had to tell her how much her journal meant to me. I also had the less plausible thought that we'd start conversations between Muslims and non-Muslims: so many of us are thrown here, adrift in this curious century. We'd have a lot to say.

I didn't believe we'd do this, but the idea morphed into an image of Ms. Shari and me—once adversaries, now friends—opening an information booth. And one day, without knowing what I'd do, I went back to the school of broken clocks to see if I could find her. The head of the department was on sabbatical. Nicole had left to direct admissions at a private school. The registrar, speaking through an assistant in a sari, said it was a policy not to release addresses: I was on my own.

From something Ms. Shari wrote, I guessed she lived in a part of the city called the spice streets because it was inhabited largely by Indians and Muslims. I went to this section, which was crowded with women in chadors, men wearing business suits and stands filled with fruit and vegetables. The more I walked there the more I understood the information center was pure chimera as were the chances of finding Ms. Shari. So when I did see her, carrying a briefcase with one hand, holding a two-year-old with the other, I felt shock and unspeakable fear. Ms. Shari gave me a direct look, clear as rainwater. Then she walked away. The look signaled something irrevocable: I imagined seeing me was something she thought might happen. It was minor, but satisfying, the way it feels when a horizontal letter in a crossword puzzle jibes with a vertical word.

I kept walking in the opposite direction, passing meat shops, tea parlors, walking without purpose, until I remembered the night when I thought about decorating my hands with henna. At first it was a memory. Then it became a desire. Women I asked about henna shook their heads. A man unloading a crate of apples overheard me. "It's private," he said. "Women do it together here. But someone from Turkey has a parlor around the corner. They call her the henna artist."

The parlor was dark with red pillows, pillows I'd imagined in Ms. Shari's house, except the room was filled with western teenagers. The henna artist wore modern slacks and crescent earrings. "Do you want a traditional design or a modern one?" she asked. "Traditional," I said. She worked with terse efficiency. At one point she told me about a woman in her village whose husband left her for a month. This woman gathered eleven friends and read the Koran backwards by the light of a full moon. As soon as they'd finished reading her husband came home. I wondered if she knew I wasn't happy about my divorce and was giving me advice. But she looked at me sharply and said, "It was a coincidence, in my opinion."

When the thick clay mixture dried, my hands looked like those of Ms. Shari and the representative, as well as the hands of many other women on the spice streets. The dots on my fingers were fertile, sprouting innumerable gardens: there were garlands around my wrists, flowers on my forearm. These hands could hold a pen, drive a car, make a meal. They could morph into deities of anger and protection. Indeed, if you looked at my hands alone, you'd never guess who I was or where I came from. And then, with surprise beyond fear, I saw Ms. Shari and her child walking to catch a bus a block from the parlor. It was an accident outside of a puzzle. The collision made both of us smile. Ms. Shari told me the name of her son. I showed her the patterns on my hands.

Misha Gordin

Misha Gordin

Misha Gordin

Misha Gordin

Misha Gordin

Jeff Holt

The Harvest

A stranger's planting seeds in parts of me,
Staking his claim in my internal land.
He turns his spade; I twist in agony.
I pray that he will tire and rest his hand.

At first the stranger dug within my breast.
A lump arose, the first fruit of his crop.
He left it there. Never content to rest,
He moved into my lungs. He will not stop

Until he's drained my soil of nutrients.
To him, my organs are just ripening.
He doesn't know he toils at my expense;
I'm just a field that he is harvesting.

R.S. Gwynn

Release

Slow for the sake of flowers as they turn
    Toward sunlight, graceful as a line of sail
        Coming into the wind. Slow for the mill-
Wheel's heft and plummet, for the chug and churn
    Of water as it gathers, for the frail
        Half-life of spraylets as they toss and spill.

For all that lags and eases, all that shows
    The winding-downward and diminished scale
        Of days declining to a twilit chill,
Breathe quietly, release into repose:
        Be still.

R.S. Gwynn

The Debt

He is the one you wouldn't care to know.
He takes your arm with damp, fish-smelling hands
And gives no clue when he intends to go.
After an hour or so, he makes demands
That everyone must leave, and so they do.
The clock chimes midnight faintly, and you find
No company around but him and you.
He claims he has a need to speak his mind.
The first thing he reveals is what you own;
The second, how you shall be made to pay
For everything you thought you bought so cheap.
There in that chilly room, beside a heap
Of crumpled papers, you two sit alone.
He tilts his glass, and settles in to stay.

Rachel Hadas

Looking Forward

The time ahead
shrinks as we look,
shrinks whether we
look or not.
We look forward
to the fact
that what is happening
as we speak
will soon recede.
This backward-tugging
current toward
oblivion can
be counted on
as one depends
upon a drug
to kick in soon—
sooner, please!
"Half in love with easeful"—
not exactly.
Call it a proleptic
pang of gratitude
for what, when it finally
arrives, we can hardly
wait to fade.
Our stubborn impatience,
our hurry to be done with
comes coupled with a cloudy
zest for any outcome.
The idea
of a beginning
is the beginning
of an end.

Rachel Hadas

Black Coat, Blue Lake

We picked Death's pockets, Charlie, you and I,
And turned them inside out triumphantly,
And got away,
Retrieving the shared essence of the day:

One morning purloined from the long black coat
You'd huddled in through winters in New York
And now, beyond
The reach of weather, wore. Or was that Death

Gauntly flapping in the ankle-length
Black wrap? You looked like Death,
A little. Who
Doesn't? The pockets all were empty—that

I know, even if I'm not sure whose they were.
Our hands as quick as lightning in and out
Burrowed, rummaged,
Emerging cold and empty, so we spread them

Out in the sun, shook them as if to dry,
Our twenty fingers wiggling as one.
We might have rolled
In the wet grass, but there was no more time

Keep moving! So you took the wheel again
And we resumed our circumnavigation
Around the blue
Eye of the phantom lake. Defiant joy:

Why not name it now? For there we were.
The sun got high, and you peeled off the dank
Coat, handed it
To poor skinny shivering Death to wear.

Dolores Hayden

The Language of Flowers

The career of flowers differs from ours
only in audibleness.
      —Emily Dickinson

Affection jonquils can bespeak,
red tulips, *Love*. Strategic, meek,

she shears some lilies for her carafe,
adds jasmine sprays to telegraph

hesitant *Sensuality*,
plan pleasures neighbors need not see.

A full-blown rose, *Meet Me Tonight*,
placed over two buds, warns *Secret Flight*.

Lush honeysuckle may confuse,
since *Bonds of Love* might still refuse

if she's twined sprigs of dark green holly,
Foresight, with columbine for *Folly*.

And if some love has proven false,
fallen for one of her friends, or worse . . .

it's lobelia, *Malevolence*,
dark-stemmed blue buds, small ones. She's tense,

troubled, teary with dismay.
She adds no card to this bouquet,

dead leaves spell *Melancholy*, season
favors sour whortleberry, *Treason*.

Beth Houston

Heart Attack

Her outgrown closet then too cramped for rage,
She learned escape, screamed silence to crisp air,
Trees, river filling with leaves. . . . Fall's last flare
She found jeweled in one rose's lacey cage
Of frost; she stooped, examined this new stage
So sharp its flame burned through her icy glare;
Her jungle anger, all its spit and swear,
Cooled to wit and jewels they call her Ice Age.
Even now, her last day blessed with a flood
Of roses, only one closed flower will do,
One last bud clinging to color like blood
Flowing from its thorn, her old heart's issue,
Love held so deep, so cold, that stillborn bud
In ice, that wound's child clutching one fist, two.

Beth Houston

Good Seed

The deed committed must have sown the seed
Of selfishness; if primal greed can thrust
Us into treason, deeper driven lust
For light could raise us, sprouting, groping weed.
My cells confess each season yields this creed
With shocking art despite my lack of trust:
I kill for crusts, my thirst roots through thick dust,
While bees seed breezy thoughts, sex flowers, feed. . . .
What's wrong with picture-perfect paradise
Is reason's brute force cannot check disease,
Or life's tease. Standing, reaching . . . Fruits entice
And sate growth's foreign needs, yet fail to please.
For exile's passage home, we pay full price:
Small change of deaths we count out on our knees.

Mark Jarman

Unholy Sonnet

First he refused to save himself by truck,
Saying that God would rescue him in time.
He trusted Him as some men trust their luck,
He said, and watched the rising water climb
His porch steps, as his neighbors drove away.
Next he declined the safety of a boat
That drew up beside his attic window bay.
His faith, he said, would help him keep afloat.
At last, as he was standing on his roof,
A chopper hovered close and dropped a ladder.
He shouted, "Jesus saves!" and waved it off.
Drowned and in heaven, when he asked the Lord
Why he was sent no savior, he was told,
"I sent the truck, the boat, the helicopter . . ."

Mark Jarman

Short Drill

Go pity someone. On the median
      The man with cardboard sign has company.
Three cop cars stop with celebrating lights
And the traffic which sped by is interested.
      Now, you figure, he's no longer lonely.

So, pity something as you do yourself.
      The eyes set deep by late hours in your wife,
The boredom and fatigue of work without
Believing it will ever be enough,
      Except to be more work, for all your life.

Pity the eyes, your children's eyes, that watch you
      With a green love the world will eat like fruit.
And think of all you'd like to say to God
If He were here, your bespoke deity,
      Who cannot come but sends a substitute.

Pity the air that stuffed its cheeks with summer.
      Pity the earth, warmed down to its bedrock.
Pity the winter that cannot resist
And has no one to turn to when it kills.
      Pity the tilting planet and its shock.

Yes, pity the shock. So many deaths by morning,
      So many spiders, beetles, fireflies,
Husks that have left their egg sacks dangling,
And then the day returning without pity
      With its inhumanity and human eyes.

Julie Kane

Thoughtball Villanelle

Suppose we don't need sound to talk—
suppose that nutcase Swedenborg
was right that angels banter not

in language but in balls of thought
wafting about like pollen spores
because they don't need sound to talk?

Think how in dreams our dialogue
flashes from mind to mind before
it's voiced, communicated not

in language, but its building-blocks:
Chinese-poem metaphors
ideogrammed to the brain, not talked.

Who needs the *langue d'oeil* or *d'oc*
when we (like modern troubadours)
strum on lutelike keyboards not

quite sentences or finished thoughts
but runic clusters, bluesy chords
understood (though apart from talk)
like angel banter they can't be not.

Julie Carter

Insulin

So do these numbers mean your blood is sweet?
Four times as sweet as mine when I last checked.
And do they mean you have no use for feet,
or sight, or healing wounds? But I suspect
statistics are more lies than truth in this.
For once I tasted of your bloodied lip,
ate copper's tang with every hungry kiss,
then felt the wound with aspen fingertips.

Rose Kelleher

From Schoolgirl Sonnets

The Devil

Blushing from horn to hoof, he smiles and strokes
his dark vandyke. Against those damson lips,
his big white teeth are dazzling, though he smokes.
He burns for you. You see it in his eyes,

that telling tuft of fur between his thighs,
the way he vamps. He uses brilliantine
to give his widow's peak that blue-black sheen,
but never wears a stitch, his little nips

permanently exposed. He's smooth as wine,
the kind that warms the drinker going down,
down to the grooves that join his narrow hips.
His legs are strong, his lap, angora-lined;

his tail's a leathery, prehensile whip
tipped with a tiny tapered valentine.

Tarzan

Burroughs stumbled on it unawares,
too busy worshipping his male ideal
to notice: the peculiar trait that snares
a woman's heart, that makes us melt, the real

reason we envy Jane. It's not the pecs,
the lion-killing prowess, or the lure
of Greystoke Manor. It's akin to sex,
but simultaneously less and more:

the thrill of all he's not. The speechless creature
emerging from the dark uncloaked, unshod,
untouched, untaught by any other teacher;
the babe in the woods behind the forest god

regarding us with innocent surprise,
a startling emptiness in his round eyes.

Robin Kemp

Sacred Heart

Here is the sacred heart, from which we bleed
our passions, cut lengthwise for your best view:
its chambers, laid open; its veins feed
used life to be recycled back from blue
to red, the sign of breath that filters in
and rides the pressure wave of every pulse
to body's farthest reaches; oxygen
is borne to brain. Now, watch the heart convulse
as Cupid's arrow spears the fleshy grain
between the caul and chamber: here, the barb
pushed through the other side would bring less pain
than would pulling it out, once struck. The garb
of scientific distance cannot dress
the vessels' exposed endings, though we press.

X.J. Kennedy

The Seven Deadly Virtues

Constancy

Strict constancy's an overrated virtue:
A little flexibility can't hurt you.

Generosity

While greedy bastards grab bucks by the fistful,
The generous grow poorer and look wistful.

Chastity

Spurning forbidden fruit—peel, pulp, and juice—
The chaste know peace, but rarely reproduce.

Good Cheer

When grief and gloom are what you want, good cheer
Is nothing but a big pain in the rear.

Modesty

Though sometimes modesty's worth emulation,
It's worse than useless during copulation.

Sobriety

A certain charm inheres in strict sobriety
Until one ventures forth into society.

Humility

When talk is soft, there's no harm in the humble
Who, when shrill protest's called for, merely mumble.

Len Krisak

Versed

Abandoned by the river where it stood,
All rust-brown brick and random, shattered glass,
The mill played live-or-die. But left for good
Or ill by town, I could not hope to know;
I only saw that time had come to pass,
And water ran beside that hulk, to flow
Downstream where waters seem to want to go.
Through rows of broken windows, winds blew in
And out; they made the sound that I supposed
The past would make in us when what has been
Has been too much, or lasted much too long.
Still, nothing made me wish those windows closed,
And nothing made me want to still such song
As I stood dwelling on. And was that wrong?

Len Krisak

Breakthrough

Their presence valued more because unbidden,
A few green blades appeared today where snow
Had lain and kept the fine, sparse grasses hidden.
First seen of all the yard: a patch down low;
A dead spot lying where the sun, all week,
Had shone through limbs and surely, slowly grown.
So small those scattered threads could barely peek,
They waited there to bristle on their own,
Till more would show, by then announced. To watch
This coming stubble start to fill my lawn
The way my father's good-night beard would scratch,
I waited fifty years. To hear it speak,
I let it come, like memory rough-sawn,
And push through snow so pale it was his cheek.

Louise Labé

Sonnet 16

After a time in which thunder and hail
have beaten the mountains—the Caucasian height—
a fine day comes, and they're clothed again in light.
When Phoebus has covered the land with his circling trail,
he dives to the ocean again, and his sister, pale
with her pointed crown, moves back into our sight.
When the Parthian warrior has spent some time in the fight,
he loosens his bow and turns from his travail.
When I saw you plaintive once, I consoled you, though
that provoked my fire, which was burning slow.
But now that you have given me your embrace
and I am just at the point where you wanted me,
you have quenched your own flame in some watery place;
now it's colder than my own could ever be.

— *Translated from the French of Louise Labé*
  by Annie Finch

Lyn Lifshin

When I See "Flora"

for Alma Karmina

How can I not
think flowers?

Though I know no
Spanish, I connect
it with flowers

crimson petals
opening often at night

for the dream child,
her licorice hair,
a river of night,

a rose and lily glow.
She is waiting
like a poem wild

to hold the ones waiting
for her to take them
where without

her smile of sun
and roses they could
only dream

night would go.

Üzeyir Lokman Çayci (Gorev-K)

Üzeyir Lokman Çayci (DES 14AV)

April Lindner

Our Lady of Perpetual Help

The burnt church up the street yawns to the sky,
its empty windows edged in soot, its portals
boarded up and slathered with graffiti,
oily layers, urgent but illegible.
All that can be plundered has been, all
but the carapace—the hollow bell tower,
the fieldstone box that once served as a nave.
The tidy row of homes that line this block
have tended lawns and scalloped bathtub shrines.
Each front porch holds a chair where no one sits.
Those who live here triple lock their doors
day and night. Some mornings they step out
to find a smoking car stripped to its skeleton
abandoned at the curb. Most afternoons
the street is still but for a mourning dove
and gangs of pigeons picking through the grass.
Our Lady of Perpetual Help is gray,
a dead incisor in a wary smile.
A crevice in her wall allows a glimpse
into the chancel, where a sodden mattress
and dirty blanket indicate that someone
finds this place a sanctuary still,
takes his rest here, held and held apart
from passers by, their cruelties and their kindnesses,
watched over by the night's blind congregation,
by the blank eyes of a concrete saint.

Thomas David Lisk

Dust, No Wind

Your mind is full of things you can't control.
If only you could drift in dreams. You toss.
On another continent a rose unfolds.
You stare across the ceiling, feeling lost.

A soldier lays her rifle on the ground.
Others clatter bullets in a bucket.
You curl up on your bed as if on frozen ground.
A woman ducks a slap and seems to smirk.

You twist and writhe. The blanket squirms.
Children eat who have not fed for weeks.
You rise to drain your bladder one more time.
Sleep slips away, beat by beat.

All across the starving world, as deserts
creep, a gentle rain begins to peck the dust.

Dennis Loney

The Interment of Another Man

I should be fixed on the preacher's words
but backhoes idle out of sight,
horseflies hum in mausoleums,
children snap their gum, bluebirds
dive and dispel the no-see-ums.
The sun is shedding little light.

And when I spied the billboard girl
in a choral spate of woolen grays
striding toward infinity,
I first surmised this somber mural
scene did not portend divinity
but was an ad for all that decays.

Delaney Lundberg

An Unholy Mess

Mike stood half-crouched, balancing a cup of hot coffee in one hand while lowering himself into the redwood porch chair. Right then he heard her. Rather, he heard the slider open and then the sound of her broom sweeping against the rough boards of the deck floor. He sighed. He had come out here specifically to get away from her.

She was muttering to herself. He couldn't quite catch what she was saying, but thought he made out the word "idolatry."

"Mrs. Moriarty," he called. "Do you think you could do the porch last, on your way out?"

"I left it for last last time, Mr. T.," she said, "and that breeze came up off the bay and blew all the dirt in my face. I better do it now while the wind's down."

She had a thick, strong body, made for work, and there was a finality in the way she moved the broom. Mike shrugged and settled back against the cushion of the chair. Her great weapon, he realized, was his own unwillingness to deal with her.

She had arrived just as he was tying on his sneakers this morning, the first day of his vacation. He heard the heavy smack of a car door shutting out front and recognized the noise at once as coming from her big battered Buick. He had forgotten momentarily that he'd asked to come out and clean the cottage one day while they were here.

Behind him somewhere, she swept aggressively, making grunting noises as she worked; it was almost as if she were down on her knees with a scrub brush. He placed the coffee on the armrest and looked across at the parched and treeless California hills, bunched up together like brown fists, a narrow blue pencil of a bay running the length of the valley below them. The particular configuration of shapes had always soothed him; this was where he felt at ease these days; that is, since Eden's death. He came over from Berkeley as often as he could, on weekends or whenever.

A little gust of wind lifted the hair off his forehead and dropped it down again with a tickle. Perhaps Mrs. Moriarty had felt it, too. Perhaps it would convince her to go back inside and sweep out the dim rooms of the cottage, leaving him to enjoy these moments when the coffee was still fragrant and the kids had not yet begun their clamor to take them out in the boat or to a beach.

Eden could have gotten rid of her easily; for Eden Mrs. Moriarty would have done anything, waxed the weeds, vacuumed the woods.

"Oh, it's a mess, it's a mess, it's an unholy mess!" She was almost singing to herself as she swept, closer and closer. Mrs. Moriarty had been a once-a-week cleaner, and then as Eden had gotten sicker, she had started coming in every day. One afternoon he had come upon the two of them standing in the laundry, Eden's forehead resting on Mrs. Moriarty's shoulder, Mrs. Moriarty making incomprehensible soothing sounds. He had felt like an intruder.

"She comforts me," Eden said when they were alone again. Of course, Mrs. Moriarty had stayed on afterwards. The kids listened to her, and she packed their lunches and cleaned up and made the dinner before she left. She would drop Kevin and Maddie off at after-school events and track the movements of the older two. Still, there was something a little off-center about her, and he wondered if the religious thing might be unsettling for the kids. He avoided being in the same room with her; he was glad that she always put on her coat and picked up her purse the minute she saw him come through the door in the evenings.

Kevin straggled out of one of the bedrooms to stand sleepily between Mike and his view of the bay. He had wrapped himself in an old blanket like an Indian squaw.

"Hello, Boy," Mike said. Kevin was the only boy and the youngest child, seven years old. His sudden appearance had the effect of annoying Mike slightly. He looked so pale and thin, peering out from the folds of the blanket.

"Hi, Dad." Then, "Hi, Cuffy," with a lilt in his voice as he spied Mrs. Moriarty. "What are you doing here?"

"How about going back to your room and getting yourself dressed?" Mike suggested as Kevin, dragging the blanket over the boards, made his way to where Mrs. Moriarty stood sweeping.

"Oh, leave him alone, Mr. T. He's only a baby," Mrs. Moriarty said.

Mike twisted around to look at her. He was about to reply when a gust of air raised a billow of dust between them.

"Magic!" Kevin said.

Mike saw Kevin's small hand clasping the hem of Mrs. Moriarty's sweater. He sighed and settled back in his chair once more. The sweeping had stopped anyway. Mrs. Moriarty was conferring with Kevin, leading him back into the bedroom. "I want to wear my Pokemon shirt," he heard Kevin say.

She was gone. He closed his eyes. On days when the wind swept down the length of the bay, you could sometimes hear the fury of the ocean breakers eight miles away. It was cool, as summer mornings so often were in this part of California, but there was no fog, just steady sun and these capricious little burst of wind. He did not hear the breakers today.

Eden had been good at getting other people to do her work for her. Not just Mrs. Moriarty, everyone. The accountant had been in love with her. At tax time he received her checkbook register as if it were a damsel's handkerchief. She would listen to the troubles of the garage mechanic and he in return would pick up her car at the house in the morning and have it back by noon, fully serviced. Even the girls used to make after-dinner tea for her and do the dishes while she sat in her chair in the dining room, sipping. Kevin's devotion to her was complete, though he had little to offer in the way of tangible service. She, in turn, favored Kevin with a special love: the last one, the boy.

Mike knew full well what it was that made people want to wait on her: an immense charm that she had long since ceased practicing on him. But that was normal in marriage. He hadn't been uniformly charming himself. Still, he wished she had let him rub her back when she was really miserable towards the end. Mrs. Moriarty had done that.

Eden had shooed him off to work, saying that he'd be happier there, and he admitted that that was where he liked to be best, in his workroom, making drawings, shutting everything else out of his mind for the time being. In that room he had figured out an intricate way to deliver a rainbow of dyes into pseudo-Persian rugs; he'd made a lot of money with that one, but the delight had always been in the moment of invention. One of the valves he had designed was up in the space shuttle.

Mrs. Moriarty was back, reclaiming her broom, and so was Kevin, dressed in shorts with an elastic waistband and his Pokemon tee shirt and carrying a button-eyed stocking monkey that he was getting too old to have a need for. She had set a bowl of corn flakes and a glass of orange juice on the picnic table for Kevin and there he sat, lifting the spoon dreamily to his mouth.

Mrs. Moriarty bought Kevin's clothes. The older girls got their own with a clothes allowance, taking the bus together downtown after school; they took care of Maddie's stuff, too. But Mrs. Moriarty took care of Kevin's, using Mike's credit card and leaving the yellow receipts on the dining room table. The khaki shorts were too big, the puckered waistline reminding Mike of a hula skirt, with the result that Kevin looked even smaller and more delicate than he was.

She sometimes used poor grammar, things like "them" for "these," and Kevin was picking up on that, too, Mike had noticed. He could feel her near his right elbow; as he looked up at her she pivoted on her broom and changed course. The irritation she produced in him was physical. He felt it particularly in the back of his neck.

Firing people at work wasn't easy, but it was something you could get up in the morning knowing you had to do, and you could do it. In the case of Mrs. Moriarty, though, it wouldn't be half as simple. She was upon him now, literally sweeping the tops of his sneaker. "Mrs. Moriarty!" he cried.

She didn't seem to hear him.

"Mrs. Moriarty, I want you to stop your sweeping until I am off the porch."

She said something under her breath again; it might have been, "I will wear my righteousness like a breastplate."

Mike stood up. "Look, just give me the broom," he said, standing face to face with her and holding his hands out.

She continued to ignore him. Exasperated, Mike grasped the broom handle with both hands and tried to wrest it from her. She was stronger than he expected; she lowered her head like a bull or a goat, and for an instant he breathed in the exhalations of her scalp, a blend of human secretions and supermarket hair products. She raised her head then suddenly and looked up at him with a prophet's ire. Her eyes were a surprisingly tender shade of green, he noted.

Mike sensed Kevin stirring behind him. He knew what this must look like; he dropped his hands to his sides and took two steps back, drawing in a breath. "Mrs. Moriarty, you're fired," he said.

She gripped the broom and held it across her chest. "You can't fire me," she said with indignation. "Only the children can fire me."

Mike heard the slider open behind him, but he did not turn. "The children don't pay you, Mrs. Moriarty," he said.

She made a snorting sound. Kevin had come close and got hold of her sweater again.

"Oh, Daddy!" This was a piteous whimper from Cimba, the second girl. He turned now to see her fighting a downward jerk of the mouth as she drew one arm around her wide-eyed little sister Maddie. Further off stood Dinah, the oldest, who contemplated him out of the cool, critical eyes of the adolescent.

"Girls, go back in the house. And take Kevin with you. This is between me and Mrs. Moriarty."

"No it isn't, Dad," said Dinah. The two younger girls looked at Dinah. None of them moved.

"Girls," he said again, but then heard with relief the heavy thud of the old car door, and turned to behold an empty porch. Good riddance, he thought.

At that moment Cimba dropped her arm from Maddie's shoulder and ran to his side. "She's got Kevin with her, Dad," she whispered.

Mrs. Moriarty was backing the old sedan out into the road, kicking up gravel and dust as she made her turn, and sure enough, Kevin's small head could be seen through the passenger-side window.

As the car sped off, an adrenal energy seized Mike's extremities and he stood, knees slightly bent, fingers extended, like a man on a basketball court, ready to move in any direction. But in point of fact, he had no idea what to do.

"She'll be back, Dad," Dinah said.

"Will she?" He was amazed at this moment at Dinah's resemblance to Eden, the slim hips, the hazel eyes, the narrow scrutiny with which she regarded him.

"If she doesn't come back, they'll go to her house, and we can go down and get him there."

"Her house? Where exactly is her house?" He had a vague idea she lived in Alameda.

"Oh, Dad. In Oakland. She brings Kevin and Maddie over to her place all the time."

"She does?"

Dinah nodded. "She takes them everywhere. Does her errands with them in the back of the car."

"Damn!" Mike said.

Without Cimba's arm around her, Maddie looked cold, like a child who's come out of the water after swimming too long.

"How old are you, Maddie?" he asked suddenly.

"Nine." Her eyes flickered up, then caught his. Cimba ran over and picked up Kevin's fallen blanket, came back and wrapped it around Maddie's shoulders.

"Nine, of course," he said, and looked at each girl in turn, running one hand through his hair. "Well, girls, we have to decide what to do." He took a few steps back and sat on the porch railing, pulling the little half-circle of girls

95

mysteriously with him. All beauties, he thought as he swept one hand across the top board of the railing and picked up a splinter like an arrow to the flesh of his thumb.

"Wait a while," Dinah said.

"You don't think he's in any danger?"

"Cuffy would never hurt Kevin, Dad," Cimba avowed. "She'd never hurt anyone."

"Let's go right now! Let's go down to Cuffy's!" Maddie broke into a squall, then stopped again immediately. There was something touching about her full cheeks, a little too heavy at the bottom to meet the strict conventions of prettiness, though she was lovely, lovely. Mike had to look away. Her blue eyes were his own. "Oh, Maddie," he said, and touched the top of her blond head, pulling her towards him.

"Look girls. Maybe we could start looking for someone new. Someone like Mrs. Moriarty, only—" he broke off. He couldn't think of any descriptive terms that fit the bill.

"But Dad, Kevin loves Cuffy," Cimba said.

"I see." Mike surveyed their young faces. "Do you all love her?"

Dinah shrugged. Cimba pursed her lips in thought. Maddie, standing close, whispered "yes" with conviction.

He went inside and they followed him. He grabbed an old phone book to look up Mrs. Moriarty's address. "2410 Balboa," he read. Dinah sat down at the laptop stationed on the desk and began typing. There wasn't a printer in the house, so she had to transcribe the Mapquest directions as he watched over her shoulder. When she was done she tore the sheet off the pad and handed it to him without comment.

He hesitated, glancing down at the instructions and then out the window towards the road. "Well," he said after a moment. "I'll go."

"We'll all go," said Cimba.

"No," Mike pronounced, firmly enough that for once no one argued with him. He picked up his keys from the table.

Maddie touched his sleeve.

"What is it, Maddie?" he asked.

"Just tell her to come back," she said.

He touched Maddie's head again. "The problem is," he said gently, "that Mrs. Moriarty and I don't seem to get along very well. I don't think she likes me very much."

"So what?" Dinah asked with a cold shrug. "Mom didn't either, half the time."

"Oh, Dinah," Cimba said with deep disapproval.

Mike decided to ignore Dinah's remark. "Call me on my cell if they show up," he said.

The three girls stood watching from the porch; the younger two waved as he pulled away.

He crossed over the bare, brown hills, gnarled bay trees growing like coarse hair in the cracks between them. He wound through the lightless redwood groves. He called the girls twice, but they had nothing to report. Dinah had made breakfast for them and they were all working on a jigsaw puzzle with Maddie.

His calls to Mrs. Moriarty went unanswered, but of course, if she were on her way home, she wouldn't be there yet. He should have equipped her with her own cell phone, but he hadn't. He continued on, crossing the bridge and skirting the Richmond oil refineries, their tanks lined up like hat boxes by the muddy San Francisco Bay.

He reached Oakland and got off the freeway in what was generally the right area. He hadn't consulted the directions up to this point; he hadn't needed to. Now he pulled off to look them over and to call the girls.

Still no word. Next he called Mrs. Moriarty's. She picked right up.

"Mrs. Moriarty, have you got Kevin there?"

"Mr. T!" she shouted into the phone.

The connection wasn't great. "Is Kevin all right?" Mike asked.

She made one of her incoherent noises, then bellowed, "Of course he is! What do you think?" This was followed by a burst of static.

"You know, Mrs. Moriarty, you can't just drive off with someone else's child."

"I made a promise to Eden, Mr. T.," came the voice of Mrs. Moriarty. "I promised I would take care of Kevin as long as he needs me. And don't tell me that you're up to the job yourself, because you're not."

He sighed. "All you really had to do was give me the broom, Mrs. Moriarty," he said.

"You could call me Cuffy, like they do."

"I'll be there in a few minutes."

"We're not going anywhere. Here, Kevin wants to say hello."

"Hi, Dad." It was Kevin's voice, clear as a bell.

"Hang on, Kevin. I'm on my way."

But Mrs. Moriarty had already grabbed the phone back. "No rush!" she

97

cried.

As he clicked the phone off, he looked around at where he was and experienced a small shiver of recognition. He pulled out into the traffic then, reversed direction, and following his nose, made his way to a pair of tall inswung iron gates.

St. Agnes Cemetery. He'd been there twice. Once on the day of the funeral, of course, and once a few days before. It was that first day he remembered best. Eden was dead and they hadn't done anything about a burial plot, hadn't even discussed it. Eden's mother, who flew out for the very end, was furious at him, at everything he'd done and hadn't done. He and she drove all over the East Bay that morning, looking at cemeteries. Her face as hard as stone, she acted like a woman buying a ball gown. Nothing would do. They ended up here, exhausted, neither one caring so much anymore what they found.

He had never been back since the funeral, and all he could remember of that day was the unbearable pain of looking into Maddie's face. Had Kevin even been there? Yes, he had, his head buried in Mrs. Moriarty's coat.

Was it madness to go and stand by that grave before he pushed on to Mrs. Moriarty's? He had heard from someone that Eden's mother had bought a very posh headstone. Maybe that was part of what had kept him away.

But he should have come before. He should have brought the kids. He'd been remiss in so many ways, more than even Eden's mother could count.

He drove in, parked, and crossed the dry grass, past an ugly white mausoleum overhung with ungainly eucalyptus trees. A single older man knelt by another grave at a distance; otherwise the place was deserted. He quickly found the stone: Eden Tybie, Wife and Mother, and the dates.

The stone looked more like limestone than granite. A low relief of Jesus emerged from its surface, holding a cross in one arm and a lamb in the other. Three more lambs lay at his feet. The lamb that he held had a small pair of horns; the others did not. It was his family, Mike saw: one little boy and the three girls.

He couldn't bear to look at it. He crouched down quickly, lowering his head. Grasping two clumps of grass on either side of the stone, he abruptly tore them out by the roots. She'd done it again, he thought; she'd given other people all the work. "Oh, Eden," he whispered through his teeth. "Just look at the mess you've left behind."

He stood and found himself not crying, but shaking all over, still holding the two tufts of grass in his hands.

He raised his head and caught sight of the other mourner, still kneeling as before, the very image of ordinary, respectable grief. Mike envied him. Right now, if he could locate a stick of dynamite, he'd bury it up to the fuse, light it and blow himself and what remained of Eden to fine particles of dust. Let Eden's mother and Mrs. Moriarty sort the rest of it out.

The feeling passed. Unbidden, then, Maddie's bereft face appeared before him in his mind's eye. The sight of it caused him to kneel down remorsefully and pat the clumps of grass back into place. Maddie, Cimba, Dinah, all before him now, gazing in reproach. And where was Kevin? He couldn't even will himself to summon up the image.

But out of that empty place came a certainty that he couldn't fire Mrs. Moriarty. Not yet, at least. What a mess, what a mess, what an unholy mess.

She lived, he discovered, in a single story house half hidden behind a mass of lank camellia bushes. The property as a whole was in great need of attention. Was there a Mr. Moriarty? He had never heard of one.

Mrs. Moriarty answered the door. There was no great defiance in her manner. Maddeningly, she was just the way she always was.

"Where is he?" Mike asked.

"He's in the TV room," she said, gesturing towards one of the doorways that led from the hall they were standing in. "Watching Pokemon."

"I just want to take him home now, Mrs. Moriarty. You and I can talk later."

"You know, Mr. T., I don't know if he's ready to go with you just yet." She took one step closer to him, and Mike began to imagine an awful scene taking shape, with Kevin in the role of the broom. But she stopped where she was, looking up into his face with an intimacy that he knew he would have to resign himself to for the time being. "Why don't we let him choose?" she asked boldly.

"Choose?" Mike repeated. How had he come to a place where his son might choose to come home with him, or might choose not to?

"I'll get him," she said, and moved off towards the toneless cartoon music in the other room, calling Kevin's name. But she re-emerged after a moment alone. "He only wants to go with you if you'll promise him you'll keep me on."

"He said that?"

"He did, Mr. T. And if you're smart, you'll see that it's going to work best if he goes with you because he wants to, because he knows everything's going

99

to be all right."

At this moment Kevin edged through the doorway in his ridiculous over-sized shorts. Mike felt the urge to avert his eyes, as he had from the tombstone.

Coward though he might be, he knew that Mrs. Moriarty was right. In a way, entering into mortal combat with her would have been easier. Now he saw how much of it was up to him alone.

Ahead lay the day when Kevin would judge him, most likely very harshly. But it could not be today. Today, when Kevin might well choose against him, Mike knew he must protect the boy from such a choice. For a start, Mike needed to raise his eyes and look at this son of his.

Marge Lurie

Promises

Her eyes are bulging, and she is hissing like a snake: "That bitch, she is trying to kill me," and my father is saying "Rita, calm yourself," but she cannot be calmed, not now, at 84, in this place with people whose eyes no longer focus and whose mouths no longer contain their drool, creeping along like four-legged creatures on walkers, while she is pitched in a fight for survival, a fight she will not remember in a minute, though certain things are still intact after all—so that when her husband of 61 years says, "Rita you are showing great fortitude," she considers the statement and says, perhaps "three-i-tude," and he, for his part, is blinded by her brilliance, that still-sharp wit, after all the ravages of this disease that has no cure.

But then it is feeding time, and his wife, who once drilled into her daughters table manners worthy of a visiting dignitary, lunges at the food, grabs a slippery peach out of a bowl with both hands, eats half, and throws the other half on the floor, giving it a two thumbs down. "It's swill," she says.

And then the tantrum is over, and what takes its place is fear, and she looks at me with what seems to me to be a kind of resignation, the resignation of knowing your care is now in someone else's hands, and she says, "Am I going to die in here?" and I, her daughter, say "no," remembering all the times she has assured me of things that one cannot be assured of. "No, I promise," I say and then she lets me stroke her papery cheek, the one that is closest.

Amit Majmudar

Balloons

Barefoot the children are running, their fists in the air.
They laugh a ticklish laughter, not the mind's.
The strings they clutch are as thin as the air at this altitude.
What are they running from? Ask a forget-me-not.
Sunflowers read their passage from west to east.
The flowers are foreground: beyond them, the precipice.
A broom of a wind swishes across a footprint.
That little piggy was hearing, that little piggy was vision. . . .

Decades, decades after my mother created me,
I make her a metaphor, an image to hear
In which the young are the old, and the bodies are minds.
She forgets she was listening just as I tell her the children
Have opened their hands. Time to say bye. The balloons,
Faceless and empty, are nodding their heads in ascent.

Molly Malone

Seal

He still hasn't talked to us yet. It's been about two weeks since they dropped him off. I don't really see him much, with school and all, I'm only really home to do homework and leave again, but I wonder about him. Not really worry— no, I don't tend to worry about anything—but I do wonder.

He has this seal that he drags around with him everywhere and, from the way he looks at it, I wonder if he talks to that little dirty white toy more than he talks to people.

Last night I walked up to bed around midnight. My arms were full of chemistry books; I was walking really slowly so I wouldn't bump something and drop them. His door was open just a crack—he always insisted on that— and I heard noises from inside. He was talking.

I knew it must be him because there wasn't anyone else who could be in there at this time of night, but of course I didn't recognize his voice. I'd never heard it.

"I don't want to like it here, Mike," he said. I leaned against the wall, try- ing to get a good view of his bed through the crack without letting him see me. "Help me not to like it. We can talk about all the bad parts." I finally wedged myself against the linen closet door so that, if I squinted and twisted my head sideways, I could see him bundled in blankets against his headboard, holding that old stuffed seal in both hands. He was frowning at it, as if listen- ing intently. When he spoke again, I knew he was answering whatever it was that the silent creature had said.

"Yeah, they do make chicken a lot, and we don't like chicken, do we? And bedtime is kind of early. And, and—" He let out a long sigh and closed his eyes. The way he leaned his head back against the headboard made me think of someone far older than his six years. I slipped into my room and set my books down on my desk. His small, serious voice kept reverberating in my head. "I don't want to like it here, Mike."

103

"Why not?" I whispered. Suddenly, it was very, very important that he like it here. I was desperate for him to love living in my house. I turned and moved quickly across the hall. He jumped when I was suddenly sitting on the end of his bed. I guess I must have looked frightening, with my mascara smeared under both eyes and my hair tortured into a tangled mop after hours of fidgeting through my studies

"Why?" I whispered again. "Why don't you want to like it here?"

He stared at me for a long time, hugging Mike tightly to his chest, his eyes large and searching. "Because," he finally whispered back, "I'm just going to leave again."

Ted McCarthy

A Painting of Saint Agnes

No one caught the beauty that went before
and after you: it fed the air like light,
invisible, life-giving. And your life,
it faded into darkness too, as might

a martyr unredeemed by others' faith.
And into view a painting of Saint Agnes
shimmers; she shares the small coals of your eyes,
that knack of distant gazing, as if kindness

was an amber where the passing life was held.
No surprise then that a dark glance can unman me
in corridor, on canvas; or those full

centuries the Church calls true and plenty
fall to a blank, when an unknown hand can scald
with paint and pain; and I, forever twenty.

Solitaire Miles (Sometimes I'm Happy)

Solitaire Miles (Our Lady Born of the Blue Flower)

Solitaire Miles (Champagne Blond)

Mebane Robertson

Ms. Brown

Ms. Brown was a sunlight girl.
She traced my heel in a whirl.
She boxed my onions, shattered my keel,
Made me feel what I couldn't feel.

Mercury-head dimes, her bright symmetry
Speckled my trout into live alchemy—
Feathered my bird and honeyed my bear
Castled my rook from here to there.

So the show would go on through weddings,
Forebodings, bleedings, and beheadings,
She worked her weeding as the catacomb dust
Sifted down over the garden of lust.

A mind of many turns, she played the bones
Stepping lightly over the watery stones.
She marked with an electric eye the bee
Of my soul pinned down for all to see.

Leslie Monsour

"That slight uncertainty which makes us sure:" Lyric Grace and the Poetry of Richard Wilbur

Richard Wilbur stands out in the latter half of the twentieth century as one of the truly great poets in English. Because his work is endowed with a thriving, generous intelligibility, his poems have real meanings; their intentions are not lost in the ungrammatical quagmire, opaque language, and haphazard constructions that have been a way of life in poetry for some time.

When a poet's work confuses, it is called "difficult." Difficult, perhaps, but, more likely, careless, unfinished, or selfish. The truth must dazzle gradually, but it must dazzle. Over the years, creative writing programs seem to have cultivated a chic opacity of strange, obscure, fantastical language, aimed at achieving some sort of hybrid experience with the poem, as if poetry were a mind-altering drug, and the poet its pusher. Richard Hugo did a great disservice when he instructed young poets, "If you want to communicate, use the telephone."

Poetry that prefers to be understood is refreshing. But luminous clarity is not all Richard Wilbur bestows on his readers. He also treats us to the natural grace of his formal stanzas. If poems were dance partners, we'd have bruised, sore feet from a good deal of what's being printed today by our small presses and literary magazines. We'd swear off dancing, or we'd do what most dancing couples have been doing for the past forty years or so—dance apart, adapting our enjoyment to our own personal moves and steps. Wilbur's fluid rhymes and rhythmically controlled meters remind us that dancing with a skillful partner is a superior delight.

Wilbur is a poet who seeks a balance in his subjects, an accommodation of mixed feelings. He is known for the ironic meditative lyric, what the Norton anthology calls, "the single perfect poem," rather than the long narrative

110

poem or extended dramatic sequence. A life-affirming philosophy, applied to poetry of refined compression and clarity, combined with metrical stanzas that rhyme, could, at a superficial glance, be mistaken for dogged optimism. Wilbur's happiness, however, is far from simple. It has gravity; it can be almost somber.

In his essay, "On My Own Work," Wilbur explains, "A good part of my work could, I suppose, be understood as a public quarrel with the aesthetics of Edgar Allan Poe." It's a complex quarrel, illustrated to some degree, in his poem, "Cottage Street, 1953" (*The Mind-Reader: New Poems. 1976*), in which Wilbur recalls, many years after her death, a saddening encounter at tea with a young Sylvia Plath, following her recently-attempted suicide (ten years prior to her "successful" one):

> It is my office to exemplify
> The published poet in his happiness,
> Thus cheering Sylvia, who has wished to die;
> But half-ashamed, and impotent to bless,
>
> I am a stupid life-guard who has found,
> Swept to his shallows by the tide, a girl
> Who, far from shore, has been immensely drowned,
> And stares through water now with eyes of pearl.

The poem ends,

> . . . Sylvia who, condemned to live,
> Shall study for a decade, as she must,
> To state at last her brilliant negative
> In poems free and helpless and unjust.

In the mid-Seventies, after the suicides of John Berryman in 1972 and Anne Sexton in 1974, American poetry seemed to be in a solipsistic thrall with brooding bitterness. Wilbur noted, "Isn't it odd that our American society, the most cosseted in human history, is now so given to petulance and dreary complaint . . . ?" A glance at Daniel Halpern's 1975 *American Poetry Anthology* gives a pretty good idea of what Wilbur must have meant, even though the copy I have includes, on the front cover, the excerpt of a diplomatically supportive statement from the ever-generous Wilbur. He is a profoundly tactful man with a gentle, unobtrusive temperament. Even dedicated detractors of formal verse don't attack him. Stanley Kunitz, who remarked in a 1977 interview, "Non-metrical verse has swept the field, so that there is no longer any real adversary from the metricians," seemed to erase this statement from his mind six years later when he introduced Richard Wilbur at a 1983 reading: "Wilbur's mind has a cleansing sanity and wit that make it possible for him to view the world, despite its burden of suffering and tragedy and evil, as a place of fortuitous joys and blessings and miracles, not the least of which is the gift of life itself." Wilbur says it best. In "On My Own Work," he describes his poems as favoring "a spirituality that is not abstracted, not dissociated and world-renouncing . . . ," having to do with "the proper relation between the tangible world and the intuitions of the spirit."

Mayflies (Harcourt, 2000), a collection of 25 original poems, in addition to a selection of translations of Dante, Molière, Baudelaire, Mallarmé, Petrov, and Cassian, is Wilbur's first volume since the 1988 publication of his Pulitzer Prize-winning *New and Collected Poems*. Again, to quote his essay, "On My Own Work," (from a book called *Poets on Poetry*, published in 1966, and reprinted in Wilbur's prose collection, *Responses*, published in 1976 by Harcourt Brace; it has reissued with additional material this year, from Story Line Press), Richard Wilbur writes, "Every poem of mine is autonomous, or feels so to me in the writing, and consists of an effort to exhaust my present sense of the subject. It is for this reason that a poem sometimes takes me years to finish."

Mayflies, therefore, is an undauntingly slim volume for the years it has taken to accumulate; the pages are pleasantly relaxed in their spaces between poems, and in the inviting compactness of each work.

The first thing we often do when picking up a new book of poems is to turn it over to see who has praised it. On the rear dust jacket of *Mayflies*, the publishers have printed the opening poem of the book, "A Barred Owl," as proof that Richard Wilbur's achievement has surpassed the need for endorsement. His poetry does it for him. ("A Barred Owl" is one of eleven poems in *Mayflies* that were published in the 1997 fine press edition, *Bone Key*, still available, from Aralia Press).

"A Barred Owl" is a poem of rhyming iambic pentameter couplets divided into two six-line stanzas. It has to do with calming a child's nighttime fears, and the artful resources required to protect the child's fragile innocence from the unsettling and harsh facts of life. When a poet is victorious, a pentameter line can be worth a thousand words. Wilbur often achieves such a victory, as in these opening couplets: "The warping night air having brought the boom/ Of an owl's voice into her darkened room,/ We tell the wakened child that all she heard/ Was an odd question from a forest bird . . . "

The owl of this poem is a barred owl, a particular breed; it is also, through Wilbur's charming interpretation of its "odd question" (which I will let the reader discover), barred from frightening the child any further; it may also be regarded as a bard owl, a poet owl, whose purpose is to present "Words, which can make our terrors bravely clear." I won't give away the closing couplet of this marvelous poem, but I will say the lines compensate "the sense of the subject" with a stark rhyme that illustrates the power of reality to overcome fantasy, even in a dream.

Wilbur's trademark is "That slight uncertainty which makes us sure," the closing line of his poem, "Advice from the Muse," from the "new" section of the 1988 *New and Collected Poems*. In the poem, his muse advises that he write,

> With facts enough, good ground for inference,
> No gross unlikelihood or major doubt,
> And, at the end, an end to all suspense.
>
> Still, something should escape us, something like
> A question one had meant to ask the dead . . .
>
> . . . Some fadings of the signal, as it were,
> A breath which, drawing closer, may obscure
> Mirror or window with a token blur—
> That slight uncertainty which makes us sure.

It's excellent advice, the best I've heard since Emily Dickinson's "Tell all the truth but tell it slant." Wilbur strives consistently to obey it.

There is ironic discreetness in the title of the poem, "For C.," which teases us into wondering if "C." is a lover from the past. This seems unlikely, and yet the poem is written in "heroic sestets," or *sesta rima* in Italian—six-line stanzas with an *abbacc* rhyme scheme, which is a slight variation on the *ababcc* form used by Shakespeare in his poem, "Venus and Adonis," and has been entered as the "Venus and Adonis Stanza" in the Princeton Encyclopedia. Furthermore, "For C." begins and unfolds as a lament for the ardent, short-lived love affair: "On such grand scale do lovers say good-bye . . . / Who part now on the dock, weighed down by grief/ And baggage, yet with something like relief " . . . At the fourth stanza, however, the poem takes a turn, when the poet discloses his lover's identity, by gratefully and slyly listing what their affair lacks in common with the others: "We are denied, my love, their fine tristesse/ And bittersweet regrets, and cannot share/ The frequent vistas of their large despair." "C." is Charlotte, Wilbur's wife of over fifty years, and the poem pays tribute to a marriage, which, ". . . though taken to be tame and staid,/ Is a wild sostenuto of the heart."

"A wild sostenuto of the heart" is unforgettable language. *Sostenuto*, a musical term, directs a musician to prolong a note beyond its full value, or to prolong the phrases of an entire passage. A "wild sostenuto" is something else; it's Richard Wilbur's passionate invention, and, no doubt, the heart is the only instrument capable of performing it. The reckless, tragic fire of impossible love is legendary and magnificently destructive, but ultimately cannot hold a candle to a marriage that lasts for decades, "A passion joined to courtesy and art/ Which has the quality of something made." Its music plays over the "fine tristesse" and "large despair" of short-lived love, and leads to the poem's finale, exalting the rapturous longevity of marriage with a host of sacred, almost funeral similes, that resound like a church organ. What began in church, ends in church. Wilbur has begun to unwind the thread that runs throughout *Mayflies*, flavoring the poems, some more strongly than others, with the realization that life, for him, is closer to its end than to its middle; that he relies upon his heart's "wild sostenuto" to sustain it beyond expectancy.

The title of the poem "Zea," Wilbur tells us in a note, "is one half of the botanical name (*Zea mays*) for Indian corn or maize," and, after the opening line of the poem, "Once their fruit is picked," we're left with half the plant; the *zea* without the *mays*. The nine haiku-form tercets of this contemplative work reflect on the aspects of what's left over after harvest . . . or what's left of life when its full contribution has been made. Wilbur depicts autumnal days "of an utter/Calm . . . ," in lines that, while adhering to the haiku's syllabics, convey a sense of unevenness, like rows of fallen cane, or the physical undoings caused by age. There is, however, a more formal aspect to these stanzas. Each tercet is wrapped in supple outer rhymes, which, like the ". . . fabric sheathing/ A gaunt stem . . . " at the conclusion, "can seem to be/ The sole thing breathing." As this breathtakingly organic union demonstrates, Wilbur is a quietly conscious, unexcelled master grafter of subject and form.

The group of poems entitled, simply, "Three Tankas" uses an ancient Japanese lyric form. The tanka precedes the haiku by several centuries, although its syllabic prosody resembles an extended haiku. The haiku's stanza of seventeen syllables comes in three lines of five, seven, and five syllables each, while the tanka continues for two more seven-syllable lines, making a stanza of thirty-one syllables. In temperament, it is like the epigram. It suits the autonomous nature of Wilbur's poems, by allowing a wide variety of subjects, while the haiku is traditionally limited to natural images and seasonal observations.

Wilbur's tankas are haiku-like glimpses of the world (raindrops falling on leaves, trick-or-treaters at the door, a field of new asters), impelled to further perception in the final two seven-syllable lines. It's as if the haiku's Zen-like passivity was not satisfying enough for Wilbur, who adopted the more venturesome tanka, to provide extra space, spare as it is, for lyric irony, without which Wilbur's poetry would fall short of his effort to exhaust his sense of the subject. Each of his fourteen-syllable distillations is a felicitous conclusion, like a sip of fine, rare brandy after a simple meal.

"A Wall in the Woods: Cummington" is a poem in two parts, each distinctively different in form, and each autonomously equal to their sum. Neither part relies on the other for connected meanings, but together, they leave the subject twice blessed.

A poet of great specificity, Wilbur locates his wall in Cummington, Massachusetts—though it could well be a timeless extension of Robert Frost's "Mending Wall," a wall which divides Frost's land from his neighbor's. Each year it falls apart a little, and must be mended, maintained, put back together. The neighbor in Frost's poem quotes the handed-down aphorism, "good fences make good neighbors," while Frost observes that, "Something there is that doesn't love a wall,/ That wants it down." He questions what the wall is for, even as he helps mend it, because he values his neighbor's good will, and the two men work in harmony to replace the large, heavy stones.

In the first part of Wilbur's poem, also in blank verse, no neighbors are left to mend the wall, yet "two whole centuries have not brought it down." It is a dry-stone wall, designed to hold together by its own gravity (cement is a sin to a dry-stone waller). "Look how with shims they made the stone weigh inward," Wilbur writes admiringly of the builders of this wall, and wonders, as Frost did, "What is it for, now that dividing neither/ Farm from farm nor field from field, it runs/ Through deep, impartial woods . . . "

One of Wilbur's earliest poems, "Caserta Garden," is dominated by a fascination with an old, forgotten wall: "None but a stranger would remark at all/ The barrier within the fractured lines./ I doubt they know it's there, or what it's for." (In the end, Wilbur, as the remarking stranger, finds comfort and fulfillment in symmetrical containment: "How beauties will grow richer walled about!" He couldn't have made a more eloquent statement in favor of metrical poetry.)

In Cummington, the stranger is once again remarking on a particular wall's purpose. This time, the wall seems to connect rather than separate. It has a sempiternal presence in the woods, no longer a mere wall, but the soul of itself, of all who descended from its builders and scattered across the land. Its appearance inspires a restful, synaesthetic composure: "It is a sort of music for the eye,/ A rugged ground bass like the bagpipe's drone/ On which the leaf-light like a chanter plays." The wall is an emblem of human thought.

The second part of "A Wall in the Woods . . . " is written in syllabic, rhyming quatrains, resembling haiku-form with an added seven-syllable line in the middle. The opening leads us on a chipmunk's wild race: "He will hear no guff/ About Jamshyd's court, this small,/ Striped, duff-colored resident/ On top of the wall,// Who, having given/ An apotropaic shriek/ Echoed by crows in heaven,/ Is off like a streak." This is a good example of Wilbur's ear for language he calls " both exalted and vulgar." In "On My Own Work," he discusses a poem in which "the language . . . is at one moment elevated and at the next colloquial or slangy," which is what we're treated to here, with "He will hear no guff/ About Jamshyd's court," in which the slangy "guff" is followed by a reference to a legendary king of Persia; and, then the next quatrain, in which after a reference to classical Greek rituals for averting evil, "apotropaic shriek," he switches to the casual, conversational, "Is off like a streak." Meanwhile, the wall, decorated in the first part with "Rosettes of lichen," evolves its own mythological and ecological system of "gap, ledge, niche/ And Cyclopean/ Passages . . . ,"and untold species of birds, plants, snails and woodlice, which dwell within the chipmunk's "long castle."

In his attempt to imagine what the little fellow is saying in a vociferous "steady chipping/ Succinctly plucked and cadenced/ As water dripping," Wilbur composes a series of spirited, homiletic speculations which elevate so endearingly the warm-blooded creature's independence and nobility atop the fortress boundary of loose stones, we're pretty nearly brought to tears with the beauty of the closing lines, when forest dweller and poet are of one mind, speaking to each other "Of the plenum, charged/ With one life through all changes,/ And of how we are enlarged/ By what estranges."

Wilbur is interested in finding the eternal in the perishable, and the wall in Cummington, Massachusetts now seems connected to every wall in human history. Dense with crumbling matter, life's electric continuum runs through it—from the fast current of a simple rodent, gloriously adapted to the settling stones, to the high-tension lives of human beings—the early builders, and the "remarking strangers." Ultimately, fur and flesh are the changing, crumbling walls that connect us and increase our being. Good walls may make good neighbors, but they also make great poems.

"This Pleasing Anxious Being" is a poem in three parts, each in one stanza of blank verse, which Wilbur spikes with subtle variations. The title is taken from a line in Thomas Gray's "Elegy Written in a Country Churchyard." Other writers have taken titles from such lines of Gray's poem as, "The paths of glory lead but to the grave," and "Far from the madding crowd's ignoble strife." Its reflections on mortality and anonymity are timeless.

The stanza from which Wilbur has taken his title is particularly apt for his sequence, which lingers on "the warm precincts of the cheerful day" that is childhood, but progresses toward dark finality, and the eventual death of the author.

> For who to dumb Forgetfulness a prey,
>   This pleasing anxious being e'er resigned,
> Left the warm precincts of the cheerful day,
>   Nor cast one longing lingering look behind?

The first poem of "This Pleasing Anxious Being" recalls in reverent tones a candlelit family dinner, a scene far-removed from what we're accustomed to nowadays, in which "Father has finished carving at the sideboard/ And Mother's hand has touched a little bell,/ So that, beside her chair, Roberta looms/ With serving bowls of yams and succotash." The poem asks its poet to "Rest for a moment in that resonance," when, as a child, he kicks impatiently under the table, wishing the dinner over so he can get on with the distractions of his games.

The second part examines a snapshot taken during a day at the beach. It opens darkly, "The shadow of whoever took the picture/ Reaches like Azrael's across the sand . . . " The subjects of the photo, who have most probably departed from life by now, are shielding their eyes and wincing "Against the sunlight and the future's glare." They are busy with their picnic, while two boys can be seen playing distractedly nearby. No one pays attention, as " . . . the surf behind them floods a rocky cove," except, at the edge of the frame, with his back to them, facing the water, a painter working on a seascape. The artist, aware of mortality, watches each wave grow and die upon itself, waiting for one he can commit to the immortal language of the canvas, " . . . a wave/ That shall in blue summation break forever." In Gray's "Elegy . . . ," the melancholy poet imagines that lives and art will pass into oblivion. Wilbur sees life (the ocean) eternalized through art.

The third, and last, poem in the sequence comes directly to terms with the subject, and, perhaps unintentionally, closer to Poe's aesthetics, when it describes a winter automobile journey as, "Wild, lashing snow, which thumps against the windshield/ Like earth tossed down upon a coffin-lid." The poem gives the year, 1928, and tells us a family is on their way to Baltimore for Christmas. "Father is driving; Mother, leaning out,/ Tracks with her flashlight beam the pavement's edge." Wilbur, born in 1921, is no doubt recalling an early memory of conscious awareness, when he describes a child, six or seven years of age, half-awake, tucked safely in the back seat, paradoxically "soothed by jingling chains" (the tires' snow chains suggest sleighbells). Then, because he served in the U. S. Army from 1943-45, Wilbur is able to foresee, in the "dark hood of the car/ Ploughing the eddied lakes . . . ," the "steady chugging of a landing craft/ Through morning mist to the bombarded shore." The poem, chugging steadily through the poet's life, arrives at the moment of his own death, imagined as a shining blizzard, seen from " . . . the bedstead at whose foot/ The world will swim and flicker and be gone."

There is none of Gray's dejection as day departs, "And leaves the world to darkness and to me." Wilbur makes an undiscouraged effort throughout the poems in *Mayflies* to stare into the deconstruction, the nothingness that awaits at the end of life, by seeking and preserving the natural order of existence, the breath and shape of things; by giving lasting meaning to what perishes in time. Some may feel the coffin-lid fits a bit too neatly, and would prefer at the end something less ordinary and expected than a deathbed scene. And yet, what other ending could there be?

"A Digression" comes away with a different manner of contemplating the void. It is made of confident iambic quatrains in steady pentameter couplets. About form, Wilbur says, "The strength of the genie comes of his being confined in a bottle." What astonishes about this poem is how easily it happens to us, how naturally it draws us into its world, and how helplessly unconscious the writer is, away from his work.

Having finished some great, scholarly study, the writer ". . . stands light-headed in the lingering clang . . . Having confided to the heavy-lipped/ Mail-box his great synoptic manuscript," then turns, and, automatically, begins to take his customary route back home, walking with " . . . the tranced rhythm of a metronome." On the way, because of the between-ideas state he's in, and the weightlessness of his briefcase, "A giddy lack of purpose fills his mind," and he wanders down a street he's never noticed. The poem goes with him, and together they find themselves nowhere in particular, with no sense of perspective or focus. The lack of any relevant direction or particular desire becomes "an obstructive storm/ Of specks and flashes that will take no form" (perhaps reminiscent of Frost's "Let chaos storm!/ Let cloud shapes swarm!/ I wait for form"), and the poet heads swiftly toward home again, "To ponder what the world's confusion meant/ When he regarded it without intent." The void, itself, becomes the writer's subject, its lack of form, an obstruction to thought or wish, as difficult to grasp as the infinite, or a genie out of the bottle.

The "obstructive storm" the writer sees is similar to the snowstorm described in "This Pleasing Anxious Being," thus, linked with a vision of death's undoing force, and, perhaps, with "Stopping by Woods on a Snowy Evening." It has been suggested that, when Frost stares into the snowy woods, and finds them "lovely, dark and deep," he's momentarily seduced by death's promise of peace. "A Digression," it seems to me, might be regarded as an urban echo of Frost's poem. When Wilbur's writer stares into the unknown, it becomes a "roiled mosaic of a teeming scrim/ That seems to have no pertinence to him," and promptly urges him to "take his bearings" and return home where life is. There, he may make something of his encounter with nothingness. Poems, it turns out, are the "promises" that must be kept, before the poet surrenders to sleep.

Pondering "what the world's confusion meant . . . ," Wilbur might have written the title poem of the book, "Mayflies," which happens in a forest animated by a swarm of insects. It is made of three intricate stanzas, whose end-rhymes, *abbacdcd*, are syncopated to the measure of their lines. The stanzas each have eight lines; three pairs of iambic pentameter, the first pair followed by a line of trimeter, the second pair, by a line of dimeter. The effect achieves a lilting, dance-like rhythm, which, of course, is not accidental.

> In somber forest, when the sun was low,
> I saw from unseen pools a mist of flies
>   In their quadrillions rise
> And animate a ragged patch of glow
> With sudden glittering—as when a crowd
>   Of stars appear
> Through a brief gap in black and driven cloud,
> One arc of their great round-dance showing clear.

Why did Wilbur choose "quadrillions" as a number, over quintillions, septillions, or octillions? There's something very apt about "quadrillions," and it doesn't take long to associate it with "quadrille," a highly regimented square dance for four couples. By the end of the stanza, the dance vocabulary establishes itself as the organizing force in the poem.

"It was no muddled swarm I witnessed," Wilbur says at the opening of the second stanza, praising the aesthetic virtues of formal patterns in the choreography of these "lifelong dancers of a day," as they "Rose two steep yards in air,/ Then slowly floated down to climb once more,/ So that they all composed a manifold/ And figured scene,/ And seemed the weavers of some cloth of gold,/ Or the fine pistons of some bright machine." His knowledge of dance, and fluency in French, allow him to find the engaging term, "*entrechats*," with which to describe the hovering flight of the insects. It refers to a ballet technique, in which a dancer's leap in air appears to be suspended by the quick, repeated crossing or beating of legs and ankles, like the fluttering of wings.

An irresistible comparison arises between "Mayflies" and "Love Calls Us to the Things of this World," a poem from Wilbur's first Pulitzer Prize-winning book, *Things of this World* (1956). The title is a quotation from Saint Augustine, and the poem's wonderfully unexpected subject is the clean laundry which has been hung out to dry on an especially brilliant morning, in the chasm between a city's apartment buildings. Instead of "In somber forest when the sun was low," the significantly younger poet is looking "Outside the open window" where "The morning air is all awash with angels;" but notice the similarity to "Mayflies" in these "clothes-lines": "Now they are rising together in calm swells . . . Now they are flying in place . . . / . . . and now of a sudden/ They swoon down into so rapt a quiet/ That nobody seems to be there."

When the mayflies, which remind the poet of clusters of stars, fade with the light, Wilbur feels himself "alone/In a life too much my own," at a loss to know what his place is in the universe, or understand the purpose for his being, until he somewhat tentatively leads himself to believe that he is "one whose task is joyfully to see/ How fair the fiats of the caller are."

The poet's sense of aloneness is like Adam's; he *is* alone . . . literally . . . in a world of mayflies and stars. When he questions the reason for his presence, his thoughts turn to the "caller," or Creator. "Fiat lux," in the Latin Bible, means, "Let there be light." The "fiats" are God's commands during the Creation, the litany of "Let there be's." "Let there be lights in the vaults of the heavens to divide the day from the night" (stars); "Let there be living creatures of each kind" (mayflies). "And God called the light Day." God calls the "fiats" what they are, "Day, Night, Heavens, Earth, Seas." The human task is to notice the fair—beautiful and just—nature of God's design. That,

"Mayflies" tells us, is why we're here.

Randall Jarrell once said that "Richard Wilbur obsessively sees, and shows, the bright side of every dark thing." The adverb is questionable, indeed, but if Wilbur has an obsession, it's the healthiest one known to psychology.

Studied carefully, however, I find "Mayflies" to be an apprehensive poem. The poet's loneliness lingers at the end, along with his uncertain conjecture about joy. The bright side Wilbur purportedly always sees is seldom shown without a shaded outline to complete its character.

"Crow's Nests" may be an exception to Jarrell's complaint, and it's my favorite poem in *Mayflies*. More than in any other, I hear Wilbur's speaking voice in it, as I read its long, halting, but fluid sentence of five flawless heroic couplets. I don't know another poet who could, with such exquisite grammar, so excitingly sustain and transform a metaphor.

"Crow's Nests," starts out about a row of deciduous trees. The ship imagery serves to reveal their change in appearance from summer to winter, which also provokes a change of mood in the poem. In summer, the trees stand blowing beyond a field, like "a great fleet of galleons," . . . "Full-rigged and swift, and to the topmost sail/ Taking their fill and pleasure of the gale." Now, "in this leafless time," stripped of the energetic possibility of raised sails, the ships, or trees, stand still in their harbor. They are neither ships nor trees anymore, but, "A roadstead full of naked mast and spar/ In which we see now where the crow's nests are." Perhaps the aging poet feels some kinship with these naked trees he imagines as schooners. A ship's crow's nest harkens back to lost adventures, to the lore of the sea; it's the place, in boys' stories, where 'Thar she blows,' 'Ship ahoy,' and 'Land ho' were cried; the place men fell from, in rough seas.

At the end, the apostrophe in "crow's nests" lets us know the ship metaphor has superseded what it set out to modify, and yet its image has intensified the trees' living presence. This is more than lyric grace; it's lyric magic.

In an interview with William Packard, the editor of *The New York Quarterly*, Richard Wilbur said, "One thing I do when I find that nothing is coming out of me, is to turn to translation—a risky thing to do, of course, because translation is easier to do than your own work . . . "

One of the luckiest beneficiaries of Wilbur's dry spells has been the 17th-century French playwright, Molière. Wilbur's translations of Molière's verse-comedies carefully preserve the arrangements of rhyme and rhythm, which are vital to the wit and meaning of the plays. By remaining faithful to the prosody of the originals, Wilbur writes, in his introduction to *The Misanthrope*, which he published in 1955, he has bridged the "great gaps between high comedy and farce, lofty dictions and ordinary talk, deep character and shallow. Again," he goes on, "while prose might preserve the thematic structure of the play, other 'musical' elements would be lost, in particular the frequently intricate arrangements of balancing half-lines, lines, couplets, quatrains, and sestets. There is no question that words, when dancing within such patterns, are not their prosaic selves, but have a wholly different mood and meaning."

Mayflies includes a translation of the prologue to Molière's *Amphitryon*, in which the messenger of the gods, Mercury, resting on a cloud, engages in a dialogue with Night, who has been passing by in her chariot, drawn through the air by two horses. Wilbur has reproduced Molière's rhyme scheme, as well as the system of *vers libres*, a 17th-century French form in which, Wilbur's note tells us, 'one is free at any moment to alter line length or rhyme pattern for expressive reasons.' This was a precursor to the 19th-century *vers libres*, and Rimbaud's revolt against all rules of French meter and rhyme, which led to free verse in English. (It's interesting to me that the French, who invented tennis, also invented tennis with the net down.)

In Wilbur's translation of Molière's prologue, Mercury must persuade Night to prolong her nocturnal darkness so that his lord, Jove, may have more time to enjoy an evening interlude with another man's wife.

> MERCURY: That you rein in your horses, check their speed,
> And thereby satisfy his amorous wishes,
> Stretching a night that's most delicious
> Into a night that's long indeed;
> That you allow his fires more time to burn,
> And stave the daylight off, lest it awaken
> The man whose place he's taken,
> And hasten his return.

The pleasure of reading Moliere is amplified in Wilbur's fluent fidelity to rhyme. This is also true in his translation of Canto XXV of *The Inferno*. With unfaltering ease, Wilbur preserves, in his iambic pentameter tercets, Dante's graceful, exacting terza rima form. This work was published previously by Ecco Press in its 1993 edition of *The Inferno*, in which several poets were invited to contribute their own translations of various Cantos (as an amusing aside, Carolyn Kizer's submission of Canto XVII, entitled, "In Hell with Virg and Dan," was rejected). In his 1994 translation of *The Inferno*, Robert Pinsky received high acclaim for preserving Dante's terza rima form, but the rhymes

Pinsky employs throughout the book are of so slant a nature, I like to call his version, "Pisa rima." The near-rhymes call attention to themselves, almost as if Pinsky had gone out of his way to reject exact ones. It's gratifying to see Wilbur's uncompromising Canto reprinted here, as a glorious reminder of the possibilities English has to offer when fully committed to rhyme.

The two Baudelaire poems that appear in *Mayflies* were originally published in 1955 in a New Directions edition of *The Flowers of Evil*. Wilbur has apparently revised his translations slightly, something he seldom does. Once again he has remained faithful to Baudelaire, who was a consummate rhymer. It has always seemed strange to me that Richard Howard's translation is so widely used in classrooms. Howard abandons the rhymes utterly, and impoverishes the experience of reading Baudelaire for the non-French-speaking student.

In *Mayflies*, "The Albatross" appears in iambic pentameter quatrains, sticking to Baudelaire's *abab* rhyme scheme. The great sea-bird, magnificently at home in the air, is a pitiful, unsightly captive on the deck of a fishing boat, mocked by ignorant fishermen. The albatross reminds the poet of himself:

> The Poet is like this monarch of the clouds,
> Familiar of storms, of stars, and of all high things;
> Exiled on earth amidst its hooting crowds,
> He cannot walk, borne down by giant wings.

The integrity of rhyme and meter in the poem are the very elements that restore the bird, or poet, to power, in the midst of his helpless plight.

Baudelaire's "Correspondences" is a sonnet, which Wilbur has translated as a Shakespearean one. It is a sensually lush poem, whose presence further extends the task in "Mayflies," for humans not only "joyfully to see," but hear, taste, smell, and touch the delights of nature.

"Sea Breeze," by Stéphane Mallarmé, seems part of the consciousness which pervades *Mayflies*, of a being who realizes life's voyage is approaching its destination. It does so with the high spirit of one who is not coming ashore, but about to embark on new voyages of discovery:

> The flesh grows weary. And books, I've read them all.
> Off, then, to where I glimpse through spray and squall
> Strange birds delighting in their unknown skies!
>
> . . . Come, ship whose masts now gently rock and sway,
> Raise anchor for a stranger world! Away!

The poet gains nerve at the end, turning from those he leaves behind to those he joins:

> In seas where many a craft has met its end,
> Dismasted, lost, with no green island near it . . .
> But hear the sailors singing, O my spirit!

Wilbur's translations perform the miracle of bringing the original fully back to life in its unchanged body, same face, same lips, same heartbeat; all the physical beauty stays. In Wilbur's hands, poetry is the universal language.

May the voice of this sure-thinking, clear-sighted poet of uncertainties, with his balanced vision of ineluctable shadow and undiscouraged shining (to borrow Auden's phrase about Freud), remain with us well into the new century. Wilbur's work embraces the rich exchange of pleasure and reward that accompanies the writing and receiving of great poetry. In his own words:

> There's nothing so wonderful as having constructed some-
> thing perfectly arbitrary, without any help from anybody else,
> out of pure delight and self-delight, and then to find out that
> it turns out to be useful to a few others. You have it both
> ways, if you're lucky: you do exactly as you want to do, you're
> as lonely and as happy as a child playing with his toy trains,
> and then it turns out that people are grateful to you . . .

Wilbur has been lucky for a very long time; he remains a predominantly lonely, happy poet, for which we, his readers, are increasingly grateful.[8]

---

[8] *The author is grateful to Timothy Steele for his valuable contribution to this article.*

Richard Moore

Metrical Reflection

Only a heedless swine
would write a headless line
and epileptic fit
move him to publish it.

Billy Monday (Arch Rock)

Billy Monday (Claire #5)

Esther Greenleaf Mürer

À la carte

The salad's bid farewell to muscle tone,
the soup sprawls apathetic in the dish,
the roast is spavined gristle, fat and bone,
the snickerdoodles aftertaste of fish.

The soup sprawls apathetic in the dish,
not caring whether it is slurped or sipped.
The snickerdoodles aftertaste of fish;
at least no one can call them nondescript.

Not caring whether it is slurped or sipped,
the wine lolls nonchalantly in the glass.
At least no one can call them nondescript
who choose to give this restaurant a pass.

The wine lolls nonchalantly in the glass
hinting at bare feet trampling out the juice.
Who choose to give this restaurant a pass
will never be accused of self-abuse.

Hinting at bare feet trampling out the juice,
the salad's bid farewell to muscle tone.
You'll never be accused of self-abuse
for shunning roasted gristle, fat and bone.

Timothy Murphy

Tête Rouge Cache

Had I a wooden ship
to bear my love from me,
I'd fire it at its slip,
then warp it out to sea.
Or must I strew his ashes
on wild Wyoming passes
climbed in the Seventies?
The thought of that abashes
me and my aching knees.
He'll sleep in prairie grasses
under his apple trees.

Queen Esther

Perhaps the most interesting bureau drawer in Ben's mother's room was her unmentionables drawer. Most of the items looked fragile, the same shade of pink, coral and dusty rose, stacked in three rows like silk scarves. Further, once the compartment was drawn open, a sweet aroma wafted out of a calico sachet bag.

Petticoats, half slips, camisoles, panties, and, at the very bottom, the ballast—a chunky girdle festooned with bone stays, wire fasteners and elastic straps with catches that kept her nylon sheers from drooping like loose skin on her legs. "It doesn't belong here," thought Ben. He recalled an aged catfish he'd once pulled out of a pond with wire leaders and hooks decorating its mouth.

Ben had looked forward to this day. She'd promised the two of them were going on a special trip. He sat all dressed on the side of the fully made bed. His father had left early to hurry onto the golf course.

"Where are we going, Ma?"

"To a Queen Esther social."

Queen Esther was the name of her Sunday Bible class. All women, most of whom Ben thought looked like boarded-up Victorian houses. His mother was the youngest and prettiest in the group. He watched her draw cocoa stockings up her legs, careful so as not to cause them to run, then roll their ends in cloth-covered rubber bands high on her thighs.

"Are the seams straight, Ben?" she asked. Lifting up the half slip.

"Yes," he said. She never asked his father.

"Ben, go get the clear nail polish."

He watched her dab its applicator brush on the snag that threatened to travel a cloud stream down her leg.

"What's a social, Ma?"

"An occasion when women get together."

"What do they do?"

130

"Oh, talk. Drink tea, and there will be much to eat." He'd seen the fresh macaroni salad sitting in a container in the refrigerator that morning.

"What will I do?"

It didn't matter, actually. When he was invited by his father to go someplace, it meant sitting on a barstool downing several fountain Coca-Colas while studying reflections of the patrons in the giant bar mirror. It was always dusky in those places, and smelled of Lysol. His father never wanted to leave. But he and his mother took long drives in the country; she'd turn on the car radio and sing like Jo Stafford. Sometimes she'd drive thirty miles to Warren, Ohio, to visit her aunt. Ben would walk down the street to the crossing and watch the freight trains move through. Alongside the tracks a black man owned a shack roofed with metal Royal Crown Cola signs; he sold bread, milk, candy, and soda chilled in an ice trough. Ben liked to go inside and "fish" for a bottle of lime green soda. The store had a dirt floor. Black children would fish with him in the soda trough, too. They liked purple soda.

"You will do what you've always done, Ben . . . stick by me."

The social was being held in a rambling Queen Anne Victorian with a grand wrap-around porch in a rural community called Harmony. Several wicker-back rocking chairs with peony cushions lined either side of the oval windowed entrance like hotel guests taking the morning sun. When the pair climbed the steps to twist the bell, Ben spotted goats in a penned enclosure alongside the driveway.

"See," she said, "I told you there would be something for you to do."

Ben immediately recognized Grace McKibben when the door opened, the president of the Queen Esther class. Except he was used to seeing her dressed in black wool, layers of it—blouse, cardigan sweater, a jacket, and skirt that fell just above a short expanse of her black cotton stockings and string-tied heels. A cameo brooch was the only color in the whole expanse of garments, and it rested tight against her Adam's apple. Mrs. McKibben always wore a pill box hat in church, too, with black netting over her chignon—a dark scrim that she might pull down over her chalky face at a moment's notice, he thought.

But this Saturday morning, she met mother and son at the door in a dress patterned with a riot of melon peonies, like those on the porch rockers' cushions, against an ivory background, and matching salmon satin slippers and hose. Stuck in her gray bun was a sprig of baby's breath.

"Welcome to Queen Esther's soirée!" exuded Mrs. McKibben.

"Oh, Grace, you look so beautiful," Ben's mother declared.

"What's a soirée?" he whispered as they were being escorted into the dimly lit vestibule.

"Shhhh," she admonished. "It's a woman's social. Now be on your best behavior."

It was a grand interior. A Matisse odalisque hung in the paneled hallway. Oriental carpets jeweled its dark parquet floors, and like young girls, huge Chinese jardinieres stood sentry at the living room entranceway. Ben could see perhaps a dozen women standing, talking to each other animatedly, all attired in muted spring dresses with white or pastel slippers. When the hostess opened the French doors, the fragrance of a sweet perfume momentarily overcame him.

"Katherine Daugherty and her Gainsborough son, Ben!' the hostess gushed. The women all turned and smiled at the pair, one of them commenting, "Oh, Katherine and Ben, we are so glad you came." Ben watched a fawn-colored Siamese cat with gas-blue eyes brush up against the shiny hose of several of the guests. Cookies and delicate pastries graced glass-topped tables throughout the grand room. At one end in a circular alcove with curved windows sat a home organ. Mrs. McKibben was the organist for the Second United Presbyterian Church.

"It looks like we're all here," the Bible class president declared. "Please sit down, ladies." Eyeing Ben standing at his mother's side—"and gentleman."

The room is as large as our downstairs, thought Ben. Tufted sofas, love seats and overstuffed chairs were backed up against oak wainscoting. Timbers lined the ceiling.

"We have some minor class business to conduct before we begin the SOI-RÉE . . ." she hesitated, and several women giggled. Ben's mother smiled innocently, not knowing anything more than he did. "But before that, I want to introduce you to my dear friend and companion."

She opened the French doors to the dining room. A diminutive woman entered, perhaps a decade younger than the hostess, with marcelled raven hair, pale skin, and wearing a watery persimmon red lipstick. Mrs. McKibben wore no make-up, except white face powder.

"Lydia Hopkins, ladies." Miss Hopkins curtseyed. The Queen Esther president grasped her hand and directed, "Go bring in the tea, dear."

The woman was as young as his mother and, Ben thought, as attractive, too. "Where's Mr. McKibben, Ma?"

Katherine Daugherty scowled.

"Who takes care of the goats?" he asked.

"Ben!" she hissed.

Miss Hopkins wore a crisp white waitress' apron over a black shirtwaist dress. Its collar, unlike Grace McKibben's, was open and exposed a flushed expanse of flesh. She had a self-effacing manner, and was given to uttering short sentences.

"Oh, you're welcome. I'm sure."

"Yes, isn't it a lovely home? Grace has such exquisite taste."

"Oh, no, I didn't bake these brownies. Grace did. She's a marvelous chef."

"Does she take care of the goats?" Ben asked.

Lydia Hopkins, who stooped over to pour tea in their bone-china cups, smiled. Katherine Daugherty grinned sheepishly.

"Oh, why are you so nosey?" She glanced up at Lydia, appealing for her understanding.

"Yes, I tend to the goats, Ben. I'll take you out to meet them later this morning."

He liked her right off. As the Queen Esther women palavered about the upcoming business of the Bible class, she'd periodically glance over at him and wink.

Soon the noise in the large room subsided. The hostess had excused herself minutes earlier, and her guests were all comfortably ensconced, waiting for the next turn of events. Ben fidgeted like it was getting stuffy.

There were occasional puddles of hushed conversation, but most of the women sat decorously mum, a few studying the sunlight filtering through the stained glass window over the double keyboard organ. When, stunningly, Grace McKibben swanned through the dining room doorway bedecked in a bottle-green velvet chapeau festooned with plastic cherries, one banana, and an orange. Throwing her arms wide, she kicked off her salmon slippers and cried:

"Welcome to Queen Esther's Soireé!"

The ladies burst into laughter that sounded more like delighted squeals.

President McKibben sat down at the organ, and broke into a rousing chorus of "Mississippi Mud."

As she furiously pedaled, and pushed and pulled at the concert stops—the living room literally swelling with brass instrumentation—an undernourished Aunt Jemima shimmied into the gathering wearing a red bandana—just like on the box of pancakes Ben loved so. Lydia Hopkins' milky white face, now marred with burnt cork, and in her hands—bones.

At the nodding of Mrs. McKibben, Lydia obliged her accompanist with a stiff one minute jig and rib-clapper percussion.

The women were in titters.

Lydia curtseyed once again. When the ringmaster held her hands high in the air, requesting silence, Ben wondered if they'd visit the goats with Lydia wearing blackface.

"Ladies," Mrs. McKibben barked, "Now for the surprise. Queen Esther's Morality Play! But you must all take part." Conspiratorially, she swept her chignon about and glared at each woman assembled. "But never breathe a word of this to any of our congregation. We've survived for thirteen years through ecclesiastical famine and scarce liturgical fortune. But the God of Mercy loves each and every one of us. Pray and be merciful, He admonishes. *And, above all, HAVE INNOCENT FUN!*"

The ladies applauded, even Ben's mother. The cat jumped up between the pair and rolled its back into his side. Ben thought the shade in the room had become rosier. As if the sky outside had begun to bleed salmon. The floral upholstered furniture . . . all of it gave off a pale carnation glow just as did the soft-hued women's dresses. The tinted flesh of the photographs hanging on the wall. The painting over the fireplace—a pink calliope unicorn. The coral bordered carpet in the grand living room with a mimosa center. Peach roses now began opening in their crystal vases, releasing their perfume. Ben, wishing he were outside with the goats, and slowly succumbing to the chamber's rising temperature.

Lydia Hopkins opened the double glass doors to the hallway, and switched on the tear-drop chandelier, illuminating a wide staircase with fanciful mahogany balusters. It was as if the women were sitting below a proscenium arch.

The audience was aroused by the sound of bells Ben had heard on horses pulling wagons for hay rides. Leather belts festooned with silver balls inside which rolled steel bearings. The straps shook several times, to announce an appearance. All eyes were fixed on the upper level of the staircase illuminated by a stained glass window.

Lydia Hopkins cried out: "QUEEN ESTHER!"

About her neck a black strap of Christmas bells, and scantily attired in a champagne brassiere, one of those catfish-hooked girdles with catches to which her black mercerized hose were fastened, and no shoes . . . her pasty flesh, mounds of it, harnessed by the unmentionables, brocaded and laced but still looking very much like saddles or straps . . . Grace McKibben held aloft two tambourines like the tablets of Moses. Each step she descended, the harness bells jangled, accompanied by a furtive glance she, Queen Esther, shot to her admiring, but noticeably embarrassed, dark-faced Lydia.

The Bible class, at first stunned, gradually effected a smattering of nervous laughter. When Grace reached the last step, they were applauding. Ben heard the goats bleating in the dooryard. Without any prodding, the auburn-haired women sitting alongside Katherine Daugherty darted into the dining room towards the back stairway. Momentarily, she, too, appeared on the upper landing, slapping her hand against a pressure cooker she'd lifted on her way though the kitchen. She wore no shoes or stockings, a purple petticoat, and had a carrot stuck in her hair.

The guests egged her on as she flounced down the steps. Soon the women were waiting in line to be the next on the illuminated stairway. The hilarity was building.

Grace McKibben and Lydia sat on carpeted Kurdistan cushions in the vestibule, clapping robustly for each grand entrance.

Another member of the Bible class (Ben recognized her as the Union Trust bank teller's wife, Sylvia Lowell) poised on the landing behind an ironing board, her dancing partner. Out and in she moved it in clipped tango fashion, to the snapping of fingers in the audience. You couldn't see her entire body until she began to do a liquid turn as she and the dancing board "male" descended the oaken stairway as partners. She wore Titian-shaded panties, and for Ben's sake, one presumed, spools of thread cellophane-taped to her nipples.

Ben had forgotten the goats. He couldn't even hear them. *Would his mother dare do it?* The women all around her were plotting, getting ready. Finally, one of the last, Katherine Daugherty rose. Ben stood up, too.

"I want to do it," he begged. She shook her head and sat him back down. The women snickered. Soon she, too, appeared at the top of the stairs in a red and white gingham tablecloth.

"*Ohhhh,*" her classmates teased, as if they were men. Katherine Daugherty held up her hand to silence the impatient, and with cunning deliberativeness, peeled the tablecloth off her body. Instead of panties, she wore a flour sack dishtowel diaper and copper wire pot scrubbers she'd strung over her breasts with kitchen twine. From behind her back she proffered an iron, and at each stair pantomimed steaming the creases out of her thighs and derriere.

The assembled stood and huzzahed. Ben heard the goats bleating. *What if Mr. McKibben comes home?* he worried.

The last member of the Queen Esther class to descend the stairs was Pastor Rose's wife, Blanche, who'd tied a length of clothesline about her upper torso and another about her waistline. To cover her bodice she'd attached labels from canned goods to the rope by clothespins. Over one breast was a Del Monte Corn label, the other—Campbell's Pork and Beans. Two clothespins held the crushed tomato labels over her pelvis, front and rear.

The congregation had finally spent itself.

Gathered closer together—huddling actually—in the center of the capacious living room, they sat with their legs folded beneath them, some on pillows, still wearing their improvised costumes, or wrapped in bed sheets that Lydia had supplied. The detritus of domesticity—sundry pans, scrubbers, iron, ironing board, clothesline, clothespins, ersatz fruit—and even silk panties, girdle and one camisole—lay in a heap over by the organ.

They ate coleslaw, macaroni salad, potato salad, and baked beans on paper plates served by Miss Hopkins, who by now had cold cream buttering her face. Coffee was perking in the huge metal church urn in the kitchen. Katherine Daugherty made a plate of food for her son, who sat off with the cat, wondering if Mr. McKibben might take him out to tend the goats. It felt like it was getting that time of day. The dusty rose atmosphere in the room had begun to give away to a chromatic blue, and the strong fragrance of lavender sachet had evaporated . . . perhaps much earlier when Ben was watching the stairway show. Shadows had converged on the room. Several of the assembled looked pale under their sheets; others shivered in their unmentionables.

Katherine Daugherty finally stood, and gathered her clothes. The rest of the Queen Esther Bible Class did likewise.

Mrs. McKibben hovered behind her. "Did you enjoy Queen Esther's soirée, son?"

"I did," he said.

"Now you won't breathe a word of it, promise?"

He nodded.

"Scout's honor?"

Ben extended his index and middle finger.

"You're still a little man. That's why your mother let you attend. We don't permit grown men in Queen Esther's Bible class."

He could understand why.

"Oh, Ben, we didn't even get to feed the goats, did we," Lydia said. "You come again. We'll do it first thing."

22

For any creature who inhabits Earth,
Except the handful who despise the sun,
The time for laboring is during day;
But when the sky illuminates its stars,
Some come back home while others nest in woods
So they may rest at least until the dawn.

And I, when glimpsing hints a gorgeous dawn
Has scattered shadows all around the earth
And stirred the animals in all the woods,
Still sigh and don't surrender to the sun;
Then while I watch the incandescent stars,
I wander crying and desiring day.

When evening chases out the brilliant day,
and our gloom has produced another's dawn,
I stare intently at the heartless stars
that once had fashioned me from conscious earth,
and curse the day on which I saw the sun,
which makes me seem like one raised in the woods.

I do not think there grazed in any woods
so cruel a creature in the night or day
as she for whom I cry in gloom and sun,
and I don't weaken with first sleep or dawn,
for though I am the mortal flesh of earth,
my firm desire comes down from the stars.

Before I turn to you, radiant stars,
or stumble into the romantic woods
to leave my body pulverized to earth,

I long to sense her pity, since one day
might still restore the years, and before dawn
enrich me through the setting of the sun.

I yearn to join her in the ebbing sun,
and let no one observe us but the stars
for just one night, and let there be no dawn
and no transforming her into green woods
as she escapes my arms, just like the day
Apollo followed her down here to Earth!

But I will lie beneath earth in dry woods,
and the day will be filled with tiny stars
before the sun arrives at that sweet dawn.

— *Translated from the Italian of Petrarch*
  by A.M. Juster

Estill Pollock

Speed of Sound

Invent the day. The cirrus tendrils miles
high over London replicate a Crick-
and-Watson spiral. Fisheye lens profiles
the sky's effect, compressed, a wide-shot trick
that squashes the horizon, pulls cowlick
clouds tight into a future weather. Days
of anticyclone spin spin-out. Clichés
of barometric Zeitgeist pepper streets
from Islington to Peckham. Take my hand:
in us a chain of circumstance completes
a journey hailed from taxis in the Strand.
In forty-four the V-2s' tons of canned
explosive showered in from Europe—bright
light, followed by the sound of rocket flight.

Aaron Poochigian

The Long Window

Yes, dear, they're precious. We were like them once,
Amnion's unwilling emigrants
Shocked by a rude shove and the cold outside.
Coo what you will, they clearly feel
That breathing air is a raw deal.
It's hard luck being washed up with the tide.

Granted, they hush when suckled from the loss
And settle down to juice and applesauce.
Colors distract them, dancing stimuli—
Numbers and letters, guns or dolls,
The faces of the animals.
Some will be happy; most will multiply,

And that's the issue. We should spell it out:
You are the certitude, and I the doubt
Wasting your time. We walk on a divide
That runs midway from either shore.
I don't get what we came here for.
Set a term—say, nine months to decide.

Jay Prefontaine

Harvest Moon

Was I so mad last night to take a knife,
my butcher knife, into the yard with me,
on hands and knees and thinking of my wife,
stab the slick grass until I couldn't see,

until I knew no harm would come to her?
I buried that blade, it seemed, a hundred times,
with her in mind, until my arm grew sore.
I lay back on the lawn, watched the moon climb.

An hour later, I crept along the hall,
knife in hand, and stopped outside our room
to watch her swollen belly rise and fall,
our baby steeped in the brine of her womb.
A little guilt seeped in. I let it bloom.
My wife slept on. I dreamed her beautiful.

Royena Rasnat (Struggling Symphony)

Royena Rasnat (Story of a Little Dream)

Royena Rasnat (Waiting)

Royena Rasnat (Cloud of Tears)

145

Royena Rasnat (There are no seven wonders of the world in the eyes of a child. There are seven million.)

Chelsea Rathburn

The Oldest Boy in First Grade

A life-sized doll in a metal chair,
he's claimed by schoolgirls for their play.
They dress him up, brush his hair,
and give him words to say.

But while he'll smile, and blink, and shout,
change expression, suck his thumb,
no magic string will pull words out,
for birth has struck him dumb.

Years from now, the girls all grown,
they'll find him in a store some day,
and if he greets them with his moan,
they'll turn their eyes away.

Jennifer Reeser

because the cut your presence

because the cut your presence is to ache
to ache {oh no one else no no one none}
but wooed so be it orderless so won
hello it means my half in heart you break
you break {but sweetly by and by mistake}
apart and and unhealing come undone
dearly departed dear but just begun
{so broken darling so: yours to remake}

since shrouds must shrouds be love be gone to bury
the cut hello that is goodbye and sad
if true minds not indeed admit to marry
{so faithful darling faithful} let me add
to we can't be and we can be together
go don't regardless what whenever whether . . .

Leslie Monsour

That's Why There Are So Many

A soft, black plum released itself
From all its branch-held kin;
It landed with a single "klop"
And opened up its skin.

The narrow slit showed amber flesh
Of glistening surprise,
Which, uncontained, spilled drop by drop,
Inviting in the flies.

But all of nature's laws and forces,
Including gravity,
Were not enough to keep it there
And let it be a tree;

For I was there to see the fruit
split open at my feet,
Inviting me before the flies
to taste its sun-warmed meat.

I took it to the kitchen sink
That idle, blind-hot day,
And rinsed it well and ate it clean,
Then threw the stone away.

Nina Schuyler

Collision

The hospital room was the size of a birdcage. Only a flimsy curtain separated me from the Russian man. His dumpy wife was visiting again, her sagging face done up in bold paint, and atop her head, a pink pillbox hat. Sure enough, the room was filling with ugly clouds of Russian.

I picked up my violin and started to play. Outside the window, I stared at the leafless black trees. Sealed shut, a matronly nurse told me: years back, a suicide. I wanted the beautiful woman who plowed her Plymouth into my car to show up. I wanted a nurse to drive a needle of morphine into my arm. I wanted to leap out the window. A moan floated by; I looked down, expecting a hole in my chest.

It was the violin. I didn't know how to play. "Baby, what can I get you?" the beautiful woman asked when she visited the first time. She felt sorry. She had her eyes closed when we collided. I said a violin. I'd had one in my car. Not mine, it belonged to the woman who'd called to say it was over. I was on my way to return it. I'd told her she played so badly it stung my ears. Maybe that's what ended it.

The Russians were shouting. The beautiful woman told me, "I usually don't like where I am." That's why she drove with her eyes closed. Now I tried it and began to drift, feeling no longer myself but Dmitri from *Brothers Karamazov*, waiting for Grushenka. She'd arrive any minute in a tight-fitting dress and a fur hat.

The front door slammed. I heard someone brush snow from a coat. I called out, and there stood Ivan in the doorway, wearing a pink hat. "You can't be saved."

Who said I wanted salvation? Only for Grushenka to say, "Shhh," her sugar breath on my face, then straddle me and pound my chest with her fists.

The Russians were fighting, louder. I opened my eyes just as the pillbox hat skidded on the floor. A slap. I rang the nurse's bell, until it screeched like an angry, injured bird.

A nurse charged into the room. She told the Russians to cut it out and me to stop messing with that violin. "Sounds like someone's dying in here."

When they wheeled out the Russian for tests, his wife peered around the curtain. She wore her hat again, but lopsided, her cheek bright pink. Plunking herself into the chair beside me, her lower lip trembled, and I hoped to God she wouldn't cry. She pointed to the violin. What the hell, she looked worse off than me.

She tucked it under her chin and began to play, music soaring around the room, then she got down on her knees and prayed. I felt my blood coursing through me, and I pushed myself up between the birdcage bars, so close I could see her make-up sparkling, just like my windshield, smashed on the street. I remembered thinking, how can a disaster look so beautiful?

Linda Spencer

Linda Spencer

153

Linda Spencer

A.E. Stallings

Cassandra

If I may have failed to follow
Your instructions, lord Apollo,
So all my harping lies unstrung,
I blame it on the human tongue.

Our speech ever was at odds
With the utterance of gods:
Tenses have no paradigm
For those translated out of time.

Perhaps mortals should rejoice
To conjugate in passive voice—
The alphabet to which I go
Is suffering, and ends in O.

Paraphrase can only worsen:
For you, there is no second person,
"I want" the same verb as "must be,"
"Love," construed as "yield to me,"

The homonym of "curse" and "give,"
No mood but the infinitive.

A.E. Stallings

"To Speke of Wo that Is in Marriage"

"It is a choreography as neat
As two folding up a laundered sheet,
The way we dance around what we would say:
Approach, meet, touch, then slowly back away.

To sweep is to know what gathers there,
Beneath the bed: sloughed cells, lost strands of hair.
To wash clothes well is to take certain pains:
The sad and sordid stories of the stains.

Although my anger may be slow to boil,
I have the smoking point of olive oil.
Every time I wield a knife, I cry.
He has become the onion of my eye.

I dwell upon, it's true. He will not linger.
When I grow cold, the ring slips from my finger."

A.E. Stallings

Autumn Botany

You who have learned your lessons know
Trees do not turn to red,
But secretly were also so,
Raging within their shade,

And underneath faience of green,
The mask of chlorophyll,
Smoldered molten gold and crimson
Long before the fall.

Behold: they burn now like love letters
Lately set ablaze,
Gilding squalid streets and gutters,
Angry to amaze.

Timothy Steele

In Montmartre Cemetery

The seated statue on Nijinsky's tomb
Depicts him in the role he thought his best—
The gentle, solitary puppet whom
A jealous impresario oppressed.
In his clown costume with its collar ruff
And tasseled cap, he rests with chin in hand,
As if conceiving he might yet pull off
The sane and independent life he planned.

Admirers have left tributes at his feet—
Notes, poems, flowers, a pair of ballet shoes—
And if they could, the stray cats from the street
Might share with him the lives they have to lose.
A gardener makes his broom rake scratch and ring,
Absorbed by fallen leaves and litter, save
When tourists ask directions, hurrying
To visit this or that illustrious grave.

Poor Heine has his crypt just yards from here.
He, on his deathbed, hearing his wife pray,
"Father, forgive his sins!" said, "Don't fret, dear.
The Lord will pardon me: It's His métier."
Though writers can, if need be, hide behind
Their works and wit, performing artists can't,
As a young King of Pop in time would find—
A man who, like Nijinsky, danced *en pointe*

And grew obsessively dissatisfied
With a face and body others turned to profit,
Whose sexual energy on stage belied
Conflicted feelings he experienced off it.

His spirit could find comfort in this place
Which holds the Paris of bohemian dreams
And high above which, like a pledge of grace,
The Mount's vast, many-domed cathedral gleams.

Death, in *Petrushka*, sets the puppet free.
By thirty, the great dancer had gone mad.
Here in the presence of his effigy,
Some say they feel the genius that he had;
Others, reflecting on his legend, trust
That any true achievement will endure
And will prove worth the anguish that it cost.
The statue, though, looks like it's not so sure.[9]

---

[9] Author's Note

When Suzanne Doyle invited me to contribute to her *Able Muse* festschrift for Turner Cassity, I thought of his excellent poems of travel and cultural meditation. Among his many admirable qualities, Cassity was ceaselessly curious about different places, times, and peoples and about the ways in which their characters and predicaments connected with or illuminated each other. Writing about Johannesburg, Sydney, Istanbul, Amsterdam, or New Orleans—or John Calvin, the Krupps, Giacomo Puccini, John Singer Sargent, or James Jones—he was never touristic or glibly allusive. He always kept his sharp but sympathetic eye on the human significance of what he described.

The poem I've written for this festschrift attempts, in its way, to do something of the same thing. Whether it succeeds is another matter; but I hope that if Cassity comes across it while surfing the Internet on Parnassus, he'll accept it for the spirit of admiration and friendship with which it was written.

Richard Wakefield

A Boy's Work

(April 1946, Sherman County, Oregon)

They sent the boy to build a fire beneath
the steel water trough after a week
of freezing fog had hung a hoary wreath
on every bud and leaf along the creek.
The men were busy at the barn with new
cold-weakened calves. The boy would have to go.
He loaded stove-wood chunks he'd split in two
until the shouldered rucksack bent him low.
In fifty strides the barn was lost—or taken.
He stood confused with cloud, more alone
than in the broad summer fields, forsaken
by or perhaps forsaking the life he'd known.
He staggered along the frozen creek a mile.
He knew the way, but in that cloud it seemed
all unfamiliar; he backtracked twice, and while
he searched, unsure, it was as if he'd dreamed
his life and now awakened cold and lost.
But then the looming rock crib marked his place
to turn, made strange beneath a coat of frost,
and then the pasture trail a wispy trace.
With no more landmarks to help him find his way
he often knelt as if in prayer to see
if he had kept the trail, until from gray
the trough emerged, a solid certainty.
He found the water solid too, so made
his feeble fire, fed the growing flame,
saw how heat and light rose up and played
against the steel. And then the horses came.
From formless white in single file appeared

the thirsty horses taking living form,
condensed from cloud, more solid as they neared.
He stroked them as they drank and felt them warm
with living heat that he had helped to save.
Their breath plumed up in clouds, more fog unfurled
into the void, and as they drank they gave
a solid, living purpose to his world.

David Stephenson

Bunker

The urge is in his blood. His family had
An air-raid shelter for atomic war;
He has unfocused memories of his dad

Unlocking it, to fiddle with the store
Of shelved and crated army surplus things
Which filled the secret world behind its door.

Now, as a man, he has foreshadowings
Which drive him to equip his own retreat
With similar supplies and furnishings:

Canned food, bottled water, a complete
Array of guns, some girlie magazines,
A case of scotch, flashlights and batteries,

A first-aid kit, gold coins, and gasoline,
All stashed within a thick-walled basement room
Beneath some stairs, its narrow doorway screened

With rubbish, like a minor pharaoh's tomb.
He monitors a vague conspiracy
Through lone-nut tracts which preach impending doom;

Through an evolving numerology
He fixes dates when dark fates will converge
And order will give way to anarchy,

And he, with his vast stockpile, will emerge
A sort of sci-fi movie overlord,
The damsel's savior and the mutant's scourge.

When each computed date goes by the board
And nothing happens, he is not depressed
Or moved to doubt his picture of the world;

He rather wonders what detail he missed
That threw his numbers off, and turns again
To pondering his esoteric texts.

As years roll by, he diligently tends
His bunker, which in anxious hours seems
An absolute on which he can depend,

The visible expression of his dreams
And faith, his certainty of things not seen.

Alan Sullivan

The Crossroad Tree

Friends are getting old; their children, married.
We're driving out for nuptials at the lake.
Childless, I feel fraudulent and harried
attending vows we never meant to take.

Fields flow past. A landmark elm appears, broken.
It must have spooked the cows that felt its thump.
In rain and thunder, rabbits rudely woken
darted from their den of shattered stump.

Grass grows green and tall around the rubble,
a wilderness where pheasants safely nest.
No mower comes, no plowblade turning stubble.
The fallen tree protects its place of rest,
but I foresee no shelter from the trouble
awaiting this unwilling wedding guest.

Marilyn L. Taylor

Mixed Signals

*Anapests and iambs create rising rhythms, while trochees
and dactyls undercut them by falling.*
                              —*Prosody handbook*

At the crest of spring,
                    something hesitates:
the magnolias droop—
                    petals, browbeaten
by relentless rain,
                    sink lethargically
to the short-haired lawn
                    spackling all of it
with unlikely snow—
                    pudgy, oversized
imitation flakes
                    manufacturing
their erotic stench,
                    thick and buttery
in the scented air—
                    bawdy versions of
the genteel clichés
                    May is famous for.

It's a fact, my love:
                    rose and hyacinth
are a mere excuse,
                    just an overture
to the main event,
                    what we're falling for
at the crest of spring.

Kamil Varga

Kamil Varga

Kamil Varga

Diane *Thiel*

History's Stories

For her song and flight, Echo is torn apart,   *art*
flung limb by singing limb.   Each valley swallows,   *allows*
her voice.   In another tale, a flame enchants   *chance*
encounters—Narcissus, who never returns,   *turns—*
her love to stone.   Rocks, caves, dens, the hollow   *hollow*
of bones become her home—the old echoes,   *O's*
that round our inner lives like the concentric   *trick*
rings inside trees, reverberate for years,   *our ears—*
Our voices rise and leave, traveling,   *raveling,   veiling*
currents across the sea, longing to reach   *each*
Atlantis, locate shapes that sounds recall—   *call*
back the world, as it was first encountered,   *heard.*

Deborah Warren

The Fortress

It's not a journal; it's a citadel
where, on a dais, on a cushioned throne
—warming his neck, I think, a little ermine—
he disposes. Marvel! He can smell
it when the housecarl brings the mail . . . a bone
that's decomposing?—"Poetasters! Vermin!
Read it and weep; oh, we know this she-troll;
she's sent us stuff before—faugh! take it hence
at once. Into the moat, or the cloaca!
We won't touch it with a ten-foot pole.
Dross! Ordure! Over the battlements
throw it now to meet its sorry maker."
Thus it goes. In my SASE
his minion then returns the poems to me.

Geraldine Connolly

Line of Crosses

A line of crosses in a Montana field
glimpsed on an early morning journey,
appear, hand-hewn, many-sized, tilted.

Some are painted, some splintered,
staggered like soldiers' rifles into dusty weeds.
Home-made crosses, boards planted

among the hay mounds, they're things
to witness that take my mind from the green
squares of summer to bombed villages.

Let the lives they might have had
gather like a river, each boy emerging
to take his place in the world, cutting logs, fishing.

Not these boards and rusty nails. Not these
hand-picked flowers that float wrecked lives away.
Not this scattered row, its grim insouciance.

Robert West

Convalescent

You told me I looked well today,
and maybe you were lying,

but every time you look my way
I do feel less like dying.

Gail White

The Glamor

Set down in prose, the Ancient Mariner
would have a moral: Please don't shoot the birds!
We would grasp every stone that undergirds
the narrative, and doubts would not occur
as to the writer's meaning. Magic words
raised demons once, but now they make no stir;
we've cut the supernatural down two-thirds.
Dorothy's in Kansas—that's all right with her.
But when *the ice, mast-high, comes floating by*
as green as emerald, or *the sun's rim dips,*
the stars rush out, at one stride comes the dark,
we touch the borders of a frosty park
where there's no sacrament nor sorcery
that was not first a sound on human lips.

Christopher Woods (Moonlit Shack)

Bob Watts

Remnants of Nature in Our Lives

A lone hawk perched above the stall and lurch
of homebound traffic down Emmaus Pike;
squirrel's scattering of seed corn on the porch,
a few hard, yellow grains still on the cob,

the rest in unread Braille beneath my feet;
mystery of meat left steaming on the stoop;
our backyard pear tree's crop of bird-pecked fruit;
and late last night, the sound of sleepless steps

becoming two deer, bending their long necks
to feed on fallen quince, while in my throat
I taste the rise of some word I can't speak,
blood-scented, hot, a predatory truth

that names me as the sum of my desires,
another hunger restless in the dark.

Giovanni Pascoli

November

Gemlike the air, the sun so bright above
you look for blossoms on the apricot trees,
recall the bitter whitethorn scent you love
and sniff the breeze.

But the whitethorn's withered, the brittle boughs
hatch their black schemes against the empty blue,
and the earth rings hollow now beneath the blows
of every shoe.

Around you, silence, but for sighs that spill
in upon every gust, from grove and wood:
frail settlements of leaves. This is the chill
summer of the dead.

— *Translated from the Italian of Giovanni Pascoli*
by Geoffrey Brock

Kim Bridgford

Eden Song

Some days she finds herself in love with all
That makes her God: the cobbled flicker of
A toad, the grass in swaths of fresh-cut smell,
The leaves, like gleams of paradise in grief,
Falling off the tree. And sometimes God
Is gone in her, small as an Easter hat
Of bloom that spoils in its aftermath to nod
Out of a vase. Even love is like that:
The silhouette that blurs itself with need
That's met and met; the caress that passes through
To the hyperbole of dawn. This greed
Can mask the anonymity of dew:
Inconsequential pearls that wet the boots,
To be scattered in what's tangled at the roots.

William Conelly

Casting Away

for Turner Cassity

What burning force
beyond the curtain
of all that's certain
draws us out from shore
into solution?

What glitter over
twilit water parses
hidebound human
parts to droplets
in an ocean,

our needs made
slight and slender
as the reeds we were
surrender to
redemptive motion . . .

CONTRIBUTORS' NOTES

Shekhar Aiyar was born in Delhi, and currently lives and works in Washington, D.C. He has degrees, in ascending order of pomposity, from Delhi University, Oxford University and Brown University. His poetry has been published in magazines and anthologies in India, Sri Lanka, England, Canada and the USA. Credits include the *Formalist*, the *Atlanta Review* and the *Avatar Review*.

John Beaton was raised in the Highlands of Scotland and lives on an acreage in Qualicum Beach on Vancouver Island, Canada, where he and his wife have raised five children. An actuary by profession, he is now retired from a career in the pensions industry. For almost four years, John was a moderator of The Deep End workshop at *Eratosphere*. His poetry has been widely published in print and on-line. It has appeared in literary and non-literary newspapers, magazines, websites, and journals, and has won poetry competitions. He is a regular spoken-word performer at Celtic events, Burns Suppers, and literary gatherings.

Kate Benedict's poetry collection is *Here from Away* (CustomWords, 2003). A new volume, *In Company*, is forthcoming in late 2011. Her poetry has been appearing in literary magazines and anthologies since 1980.

Kim Bridgford is the new director of the West Chester University Poetry Center and the West Chester University Poetry Conference. As editor of *Mezzo Cammin*, she was the founder of The *Mezzo Cammin* Women Poets Timeline Project, which was launched at the National Museum of Women in the Arts in Washington on March 27, 2010, and will eventually be the largest database of women poets in the world.

Geoffrey Brock is the author of *Weighing Light* (Ivan R. Dee, 2005), the translator of Cesare Pavese's *Disaffections: Complete Poems 1930-1950* (Copper Canyon Press, 2002), and the editor of *The FSG Book of 20th-Century Italian Poetry* (Farrar Straus and Giroux, 2011). The recipient of Stegner, NEA, Guggenheim, and Cullman Fellowships, he teaches in the MFA program at the University of Arkansas.

179

Julie Carter was born in 1971 in Appalachian Ohio and still lives there. Her work has appeared in *Mimesis*, *Umbrella*, *Snakeskin*, *OCHO*, *Raintown Review* and *Avatar Review*.

Turner Cassity was born on January 12, 1929, in Jackson, Mississippi. His most recent books were *Devils & Islands* (Swallow Press, 2007) and *Under Two Flags* (Scienter Press, 2009). He was awarded an NEA fellowship, a Michael Braude Award of the American Academy of Arts and Letters, and an Ingram Merrill Foundation Award. He died on July 26, 2009.

Üzeyir Lokman Çayci was born in 1949 in Bor, Turkey. He graduated as an Architect (Designer of Industry) from the State Academy of Fine Arts in Istanbul. He received the Eagerness award from Radio NPS, Holland, in 1999, and the Palmares award by Les Amis de Thalie in France. He is currently employed at the Center of Adult Education (AFPA).

Catherine Chandler is a graduate of McGill University, where she lectures in the Department of Translation Studies. She is the author of two chapbooks, *For No Good Reason* and *All or Nothing*. A three-time Pushcart Prize nominee and twice a finalist in the Howard Nemerov sonnet competition, she has had poems and translations from French and Spanish published in journals and anthologies in the United States, the United Kingdom, Australia, and Canada. Born in New York City and raised in Wilkes-Barre, Pennsylvania, she currently lives in Saint Lazare, Québec, with her husband. They have two children and four granddaughters.

Cally Conan-Davies drives around Australia in her van, and occasionally breaks down in remote tropical paradises where she writes poems like this one.

William Conelly's poems appear irregularly in the journals and e-zines of the United States and Britain. Holding citizenship in both countries, he works as a tutor in the latter's Open Studies Program, Warwick University, as well as a consultant and freelance editor. He resides with his wife in Warwick, England, and with his family in middle California.

Geraldine Connolly is the author of three poetry collections: *Food for the Winter*, *Province of Fire*, and *Hand of the Wind*, which was recently published by Iris Press. Her poems and articles have appeared in *Poetry*, *Shenandoah*, *The Gettysburg Review* and *The Washington Post*. She has been awarded two NEA fellowships, a Maryland Arts Council Fellowship and the Yeats Prize. She served as editor of *Poet Lore* and taught at Johns Hopkins and The Writers Center in Bethesda. She teaches currently at the University of Arizona Poetry Center and divides her time between Montana and Arizona.

Maryann Corbett is the author of two chapbooks: *Dissonance* (Scienter Press, 2009) and *Gardening in a Time of War* (Pudding House, 2007). She has been a finalist for the Morton Marr prize, a winner of the Willis Barnstone Translation Prize and the Lyric Memorial Award, and a three-time Pushcart nominee. Her poems, essays, and translations have appeared in *River Styx, Atlanta Review, The Evansville Review, The Dark Horse,* and many other journals in print and online. She lives in St. Paul and works for the Minnesota Legislature.

Daniel L. Corrie's poetry manuscript several times placed as finalist in the Whitman and Yale poetry competitions. After working at a busy job that took him away from poetry for five years, he returned to his manuscript and reassessed it. For the ensuing 15 years he has continued postponing submitting it to publishers, to improve it. His poems have appeared in *The American Scholar, Hudson Review, New Criterion, Shenandoah, Southern Review, Virginia Quarterly Review,* among others. His essay "What Is Human Time?" appeared in *The Hudson Review.* He lives on a farm in South Georgia.

Brian Culhane's *The King's Question* (Graywolf Press, 2008) won the Poetry Foundation's Emily Dickinson First Book Award. Born and raised in New York City, he was educated at City University of New York (B.A.), Columbia University (MFA), and the University of Washington (Ph.D.). His poetry has appeared in such journals as *The Hudson Review, The Paris Review,* and *The New Republic.* The recipient of fellowships from the Washington State Arts Commission and the MacDowell Colony, he lives and teaches in Seattle.

Dick Davis is currently Professor of Persian and Chair of the Department of Near Eastern Languages and Cultures at Ohio State University. He has published several books of academic works, translations from Persian, and his own poetry (most recently, *At Home and Far from Home: Poems on Iran and Persian Culture, 2009).* His most recent translation is of the 11th-century Persian romance, *Vis and Ramin* (Penguin Classics, 2009).

Andrew Dolphin is a San Diego, CA, native who enjoys being a part of the large and diverse artistic community taking part in sketch groups. His digital designs are being used in the labels for a local clothing designer. Currently he is working on constructing a web site dedicated to his artwork and photography.

Suzanne J. Doyle was born in St. Charles, Missouri, on March 3, 1953. In 1975 she graduated with honors in English from the University of California at Santa Barbara, where she studied under the poet Edgar Bowers. After being accepted to Stanford University's Creative Writing Program in the fall of 1975, she received her MA in 1978. She has published the following slim volumes of verse: *Sweeter for the Dark* (1982), *Domestic Passions* (1984), *Dangerous Beauties* (1990), and *Calypso* (2003). For more than 25 years she has made her living writing and editing for high-tech clients in Silicon Valley, California.

Kevin Durkin attended schools in West Virginia, Pennsylvania, and Germany before earning his degree in English literature from Princeton University. He has taught English in Singapore, Kitakyushu (Japan), New York City, and Washington, D.C. He has also performed in the plays of Shakespeare across America. His poems have appeared in *The New Criterion, Poetry, The Yale Review*, and elsewhere. Currently a director of communications at the University of Southern California, he resides with his wife and two daughters in Santa Monica.

Kristen Edwards is a writer living in San Francisco. She has a B.A. in Classics from the University of Virginia, and fourteen years of business experience in the high tech industry. She is currently working on a collection of short stories and her memoir, *The Way Home*.

Stephen Edgar has published seven collections of poetry, the most recent being *History of the Day* (Black Pepper Publishing, 2009). His other books include *Other Summers* (2006) and *Lost in the Foreground* (2003). In 2006 he was awarded the Philip Hodgins Memorial Medal for excellence in literature. He lives in Sydney, Australia.

Jeffrey Einboden received his Ph.D. from the University of Cambridge (Magdalene College), and is Assistant Professor in the English Department at Northern Illinois University. Einboden's research concerning Persian and Arabic translation has appeared in scholarly journals such as *Translation and Literature, Middle Eastern Literatures*, and the *Journal of Qur'anic Studies*. Co-translated with John Slater, his *The Tangled Braid: Ninety-Nine Poems by Hafiz of Shiraz* was published by Fons Vitae in 2009.

Rhina P. Espaillat was born in the Dominican Republic. She has published poetry, short stories, essays and translations in both English and Spanish in numerous journals and over fifty anthologies, as well as in her eight full-length collections and three chapbooks. Her honors include The T.S. Eliot Prize in Poetry, the Richard Wilbur Award, the May Sarton Award, two Howard Nemerov Prizes, a Lifetime Achievement in the Arts Award from Salem State College, and several honors from the Dominican Republic's Ministry of Culture. A former high school English teacher in NYC, she now lives, with her sculptor husband, Alfred Moskowitz, in Newburyport, MA, where she is active with the Powow River Poets.

Annie Finch is the author or editor of fifteen books of poetry, translation, and criticism including *Eve, Calendars, The Encyclopedia of Scotland*, and *Among the Goddesses: An Epic Libretto in Seven Dreams*. Her poetry has appeared in *Agni, Fulcrum, Kenyon Review, Paris Review, Prairie Schooner*, and *Yale Review*. Her other works include *The Body of Poetry* and *A Poet's Ear*, and music, art, theater, and opera collaborations. Her work has been shortlisted for the Foreword Poetry Book of the Year Award and honored with the Robert Fitzgerald Award. She directs the Stonecoast MFA program in creative writing at the University of Southern Maine.

Thaisa Frank's short stories have received two PEN awards, and two most recent collections, *Sleeping in Velvet* (1998) and *A Brief History of Camouflage* (1992), have been nominated for the Bay Area Book Reviewers Association Award. She is the co-author of *Finding Your Writer's Voice* (St. Martin's Press, 1994). Her work has been translated into Spanish, Portuguese, Finnish, and Polish. She is on the advisory board of UC Berkeley's post-baccalaureate program in creative writing, lectures at Occidental College in Pasadena and teaches in the graduate program at USF. Her novel, *Heidegger's Glasses,* is forthcoming from Counterpoint Press in fall, 2010.

Misha Gordin was born in 1946, and grew up among the Russian speaking population of Latvia. He graduated from technical college as aviation engineer but never worked as such, joining instead the Riga Motion Studios as a designer of equipment for special effects. In 1972 he created his first and most important concept-based image, "Confession". He instantly recognized the possibilities of the conceptual approach, and the knowledge acquired from this image became the backbone of his work over the next twenty-five years. He moved to the USA in 1974.

Terri Graham came to visual art later in life without ever having studied any art at all. It grew as an extension of her lifelong practice of writing poetry. She mostly identifies her artistic style with what French artist Jean Dubuffet describes as *art brut*, otherwise known as outsider art. Her artwork is layered in meaning and emotion but with a subtle touch intended to push the viewer to look beneath the surface of both the image and themselves.

R.S. Gwynn is the author of *No Word of Farewell: Selected Poems 1970-2000* (Story Line Press, 2000), as well as four other collections. He is the editor of the *Pocket Anthology* series from Penguin Academics/Longman and *New Expansive Poetry* (Story Line Press). He has received the Michael Braude Award for Light Verse of the American Academy of Arts and Letters. He has taught at Lamar University since 1976, and lives in Beaumont, Texas.

Rachel Hadas is Board of Governors Professor of English at the Newark campus of Rutgers University (NJ), where she has taught for many years. Her new book of poems is *The Ache of Appetite* (Copper Beech Press, 2010). She was the coeditor of *The Greek Poets: Homer to the Present* (Norton, 2009). A prose work is forthcoming in 2011 entitled *Strange Relation: A Memoir of Marriage, Dementia, and Poetry* (Paul Dry Books). She is the author of numerous books of poetry, essays, and translations.

Dolores Hayden's poems have appeared in *The Yale Review, The American Scholar, Raritan,* and *The Best American Poetry.* "Language of the Flowers" received a PSA award and was included in her collection, *American Yard* (Wordtech Communications, 2004). Her newest book, *Nymph, Dun, and Spinner*, comes out in fall, 2010. She teaches a course at Yale called Poets' Landscapes.

Jeff Holt is a licensed professional counselor who lives in Plano, TX, with his wife, Sarena, and their lovely twin daughters, Julia and Allison. His poems have been published in *A Mind Apart: Poems of Melancholy, Madness and Addiction* (Oxford University Press, 2008), *14 by 14, Sonnets: 150 Sonnets* (Evansville University Press, 2005), *Measure, The Formalist, The Texas Review, Iambs & Trochees, Pivot, Cumberland Poetry Review, Rattapallax*, and other websites and journals.

Beth Houston, MA, MFA, has taught creative writing, literature, and/or composition at San Francisco State University; University of California, Berkeley; University of California, Santa Cruz; Eckerd College; University of Central Florida; University of South Florida; University of Tampa; Polk Community College; and Manatee Community College/State College of Florida. She has published six poetry books and nearly three hundred works in literary and professional journals. Her spiritual memoir is *Born-Again Deist* (New Deism Press, 2009).

Mark Jarman's latest collection of poetry is *Epistles* (Sarabande Books, 2007). Sarabande Books will publish his new and selected poems, *Bone Fires*, in 2011. He is Centennial Professor of English at Vanderbilt University.

A.M. Juster was *Eratosphere*'s first moderator. He is the author of *Longing for Laura* (Birch Brook Press, 2001), *The Secret Language of Women* (University of Evansville Press, 2003), and *Horace's Satires* (University of Pennsylvania Press, 2008). Oxford University Press will release his translation of Tibullus' elegies in 2011. He is a three-time winner of the Howard Nemerov Sonnet Award, and his work has appeared in *The Paris Review, Southwest Review, North American Review, Light, Measure, Barrow Street* and many other journals.

Julie Kane is the author of *Jazz Funeral* (Story Line Press, 2009), winner of the 2009 Donald Justice Poetry Prize, and *Rhythm & Booze* (University of Illinois Press, 2003), a National Poetry Series winner and finalist for the 2005 Poets' Prize. She also won first prize in the 2007 Open Poetry International Sonnet Competition. A former George Bennett Fellow in Writing at Phillips Exeter Academy, New Orleans Writer-in-Residence at Tulane University, and Fulbright Lecturer at Vilnius Pedagogical University (Lithuania), she teaches at Northwestern State University in Natchitoches, Louisiana.

Rose Kelleher's first book of poetry, *Bundle o' Tinder* (Waywiser, 2008), was chosen for the 2007 Anthony Hecht Poetry Prize by Richard Wilbur. Recently, her poems have appeared or are forthcoming in *River Styx, 32 Poems, The Raintown Review* and *The Flea*. In 2009 she joined the editorial staff of *The Shit Creek Review*. A native of Massachusetts, she lives in Maryland with her husband and has worked as a technical writer and programmer, among other things.

Robin Kemp, a New Orleans native finishing her Ph.D. in poetry at Georgia State, is the author of *This Pagan Heaven* (Pecan Grove, 2009). She owns the Formalista list-serv and has published encyclopedia entries on New Formalism and the poet Turner Cassity. Her poetry appears in *New Orleans Review*, *Valparaiso Poetry Review*, *Texas Review*, and elsewhere, and has been anthologized in *Rites of Spring* (Pecan Grove), *Maple Leaf Rag III* and *IV* (Portals), and *Letters to the World: Poems from the WOM-PO Listserv* (Red Hen Press).

X.J. Kennedy's latest books are *In a Prominent Bar in Secaucus: New & Selected Poems* (Johns Hopkins University Press, 2007), *Peeping Tom's Cabin: Comic Verse* (BOA Editions, 2007), and *City Kids*, a book of poems for children (Tradewind Books, 2010). In 2009 he received the Robert Frost Medal of the Poetry Society of America.

Len Krisak is the author of *Even as We Speak* and *If Anything*, and the translator of *The Odes of Horace* in Latin and English, and *The Eclogues of Virgil*. A recipient of the Robert Penn Warren, Robert Frost, and Richard Wilbur prizes, he is a four-time champion on *Jeopardy!* His work appears in The *Hudson Review*, *The Sewanee Review*, *PN Review*, and *Measure*, among others.

Lyn Lifshin's recent books include *The Licorice Daughter: My Year with Ruffian* (Texas Review Press) and *Another Woman Who Looks Like Me* (Black Sparrow at Godine), following *Cold Comfort*, *Before it's Light*, *Desire* and *92 Rapple Drive*. She has written over 120 books and edited four anthologies. Also out recently are *Nutley Pond*, *Persephone*, *Barbaro: Beyond Brokenness*, *Lost in the Fog*, *Light at the End: The Jesus Poems*, *Ballet Madonnas*, *Katrina*, *Lost Horses*. Forthcoming are *Chiffon*, *All the Poets Who Have Touched Me Living and Dead*, *All True Especially the Lies* and *Ballroom*.

April Lindner is the author of *Jane*, a novel forthcoming from Poppy in 2010. Her poetry collection, *Skin* (Texas Tech University Press, 2002), received the Walt McDonald first book prize in 2001. She is an Associate Professor of English at Saint Joseph's University in Philadelphia.

Thomas David Lisk's poetry, fiction, essays, and journalism (news, reviews and features) have been widely published. Recent work has appeared in *Leviathan* and *Umbrella*. His published books include *These Beautiful Limits* (Parlor Press, 2006) and *Tentative List (a)* (Kitchen Press Chapbooks, 2008). *Uncles and Eels* is slated for publication in 2010. He teaches literature and occasionally journalism at North Carolina State University.

Dennis Loney's work has appeared in *32 Poems*, *Sewanee Theological Review*, *Measure*, and elsewhere. He is the Web Production Manager for *The New Republic* and lives in Washington, D.C., with his wife and daughters.

Delaney Lundberg has completed a novel and written a number of short stories. She lives with her husband in Guilford, Connecticut.

Marge Lurie's fiction has appeared in *Ep;phany: A Literary Journal*, *Pindeldyboz*, *Ducts*, *FOTE*, *Fiction Warehouse*, and *One Last Carcrash*. She earned her MFA in writing from the New School University, and has also studied at The Writers Studio in New York and the Fine Arts Work Center in Provincetown, MA. She lives in New York City.

Amit Majmudar's first book of poetry is *0°,0°* [Zero Degrees, Zero Degrees] (Northwestern University Press/TriQuarterly Books, 2009). His second book of poetry, *Heaven and Earth*, won the 2011 Donald Justice Prize. His first novella, *Azazil*, was serialized recently in *The Kenyon Review*. His first novel, *Partitions*, will be published by Macmillan (Holt) in 2011. His poetry has been featured on *Poetry Daily* several times and has appeared in *Poetry* and *The Best American Poetry* 2007.

Molly Malone is a young writer living in the Washington, D.C., area. The *Able Muse* is the first publication in which her work has appeared. She gleans inspiration from people-watching, small children, mountains, fields, and the sea.

Ted McCarthy was born in Clones, Ireland. He still lives locally and teaches in the area. His work has appeared in many publications in Ireland, Britain, the United States and Germany, where many of his early poems have been translated by the poet and novelist Gisela Noy. His first collection, *November Wedding* (Lilliput Press, 1998), won the following year's Brendan Behan Award for poetry. In 1999, he was invited to contribute to the Whoseday Book in aid of the Irish Hospice Foundation.

Solitaire Miles is a jazz vocalist and illustrator/artist living in Chicago, IL. Her artwork is mostly mixed media, incorporating oil and watercolor with digital painting and photo manipulation. She works as an illustrator for several publishing companies, and her artwork has been featured on the covers of Luna Books, as well as many anthologies and independent publications. She has just released a new jazz CD of rare standards from the 1930s and 40s, *Born to Be Blue*.

Billy Monday, a photographic artist, lives and works in the mountains of Western Maryland. Specializing in the "environmental nude," he hikes with his models from the Appalachian Trail to the lowlands around the Potomac River to seek out the dramatic locations he prefers. Occasional trips to the American West add to his repertoire. Supported by his wonderful wife of 20 years and his three children, he continues to publish and exhibit at galleries throughout his region.

Leslie Monsour, a native of Hollywood, California, grew up in Hollywood, Mexico City, Chicago, and Panama. The author of *The Alarming Beauty of the Sky* (Red Hen Press, 2005), she has also published poems, essays, and translations in such magazines as *Poetry*, *Measure*, *Iambs and Trochees*, *Mezzo Cammin*, *The Raintown Review*, *The*

Dark Horse, and *First Things*. Her work has been featured regularly on Garrison Keillor's NPR program, *The Writer's Almanac*, as well as in Poet Laureate Ted Kooser's syndicated column, *American Life in Poetry*. In 2007, she was the recipient of a Fellowship in Literature from The National Endowment for the Arts.

Richard Moore was born on September 25, 1927, in Connecticut. He published 14 books of poetry, one of which was nominated for a Pulitzer Prize. His poetry books include *The Mouse Whole: An Epic* (Negative Capability Press, 1996), *Pygmies and Pyramids* (Orchises Press, 1998), *The Naked Scarecrow* (Truman State University Press, 2000), and, most recently, *Sitting in the World* (David Robert Books, 2008). His fiction, essays, and more than 500 of his poems, were published in a great variety of magazines, including *The New Yorker*, *Atlantic*, *Harper's*, *Poetry*, *The American Poetry Review*, and *The Nation*. He died on November 8, 2009.

Esther Greenleaf Mürer lives in Philadelphia. She has been a library cataloger, indexer, and composer. She published translations of four novels by the Norwegian writer Jens Bjørneboe, and was founding editor of *Types & Shadows*, the journal of the Fellowship of Quakers in the Arts. She got serious about writing poetry when she turned 70. Since then her poetry has appeared in numerous magazines, mostly online. She was featured poet in the February 2010 issue of *The Centrifugal Eye*.

Timothy Murphy hunts in the Dakotas. His most recent book is *Beowulf, A Longman Cultural Edition* (Longman, 2007), co-translated with Alan Sullivan. *Hunter's Log* is forthcoming in 2011 from the Dakota Institute Press.

Dennis Must is the author of two short-story collections: *Oh, Don't Ask Why* (Red Hen Press, 2007) and *Banjo Grease* (Creative Arts Book Company, 2000), plus a forthcoming novel, *The World's Smallest Bible*, to be published by Red Hen Press. His plays have been performed Off Off Broadway and his fiction has appeared in numerous anthologies and literary reviews. He resides with his wife in Salem, Massachusetts.

Estill Pollock was born in Kentucky, but has lived in England for thirty years. His publications include the book cycles *Blackwater Quartet* (Kittiwake Editions, 2005) and the *Relic Environments Trilogy* (Cinnamon Press 2005, 2006, 2008). In 2011, a combined edition of the Trilogy will be published by Cinnamon Press, revised, and with poems not available in the previous collections.

Aaron Poochigian is the author of three books of verse translations—*Stung with Love: The Poems and Fragments of Sappho* (Penguin UK, 2009), Aratus' *Phaenomena* (Johns Hopkins, 2010) and Aeschylus' *Persians, Seven Against Thebes* and *Suppliants* (Johns Hopkins, 2011). His poems and translations have appeared in such newspapers and journals as *The Financial Times*, *Poems Out Loud* and *Poetry*. He lives and writes in New York City.

Jay Prefontaine was born on April 13, 1963. He received an MFA from the University of Arkansas. His fiction and poetry were published in literary magazines such as *Alabama Literary Review*, *The Laurel Review*, *The Bellingham Review*, *The Chattahoochee Review*, *Indiana Review*, *Georgetown Review* and *North Dakota Review*. He taught at the University of Arkansas, Louisiana State University in Baton Rouge and Eastern Illinois University. He died on April 9, 2010, in his home state of Maine.

Royana Rasnat lives in Bangladesh, a country where beauty lies in every corner of the land, even in the face of disaster and poverty. She captures the beauty of nature and of the people through her photography. Her main inspiration is her beloved husband, S'uhas, who has helped her understand what photography is and from whom she has learned every facet of photography.

Chelsea Rathburn's debut collection, *The Shifting Line*, won the 2005 Richard Wilbur Award. Her poems have appeared in *The Atlantic Monthly*, *Poetry*, *The New Republic*, *The Hudson Review* and other journals. The recipient of a 2009 fellowship in poetry from the National Endowment for the Arts, she lives in Atlanta with her husband, the poet James May. The *Able Muse* was one of the first publications to provide a home for her work.

Jennifer Reeser is the author of two collections published by Word Press, *An Alabaster Flask* and *Winterproof*, and of the cycle *Sonnets from the Dark Lady*. Her articles, poems, and translations of Russian and French literature appear in such journals as *The National Review*, *Poetry*, *The Dark Horse* and *Light Quarterly*, as well as in numerous anthologies, including Longman's *Introduction to Literature*, edited by X.J. Kennedy and Dana Gioia, and *Famous Poets and Poems Online*. She is the former assistant editor to *Iambs and Trochees*, and lives amid the bayous of southern Louisiana with her husband and five children.

Mebane Robertson is a poet, writer, and musician residing in Brooklyn, NY.

Nina Schuyler's novel, *The Painting*, was named a Best Book by *San Francisco Chronicle* and nominated for the Northern California Book Award. It's been translated into Chinese, Portuguese, and Serbian. She won the *Santa Clara Review's Editor's Choice Prize for Fiction 2008*, the *Big Ugly Review Short Short Contest for 2008*; and she was a finalist in the 2009 Stanford Fiction Contest. Her short stories and poems have appeared in *Fugue*, *Flash Quake*, *The Meadowland Review*, *The Battered Suitcase*, and other journals. She currently teaches creative writing at University of San Francisco's graduate program.

John Slater's poems and translations have appeared in various journals including *Canadian Literature*, *Queen's Quarterly* and *PN Review*. *The Tangled Braid: Ninety-Nine Poems by Hafiz of Shiraz*, co-translated with Jeffrey Einboden, was recently published by Fons Vitae. A first collection of his work, *Surpassing Pleasure*, is forthcoming from Porcupine's Quill in Spring, 2011. He is a Cistercian monk in upstate New York.

Linda Spencer, Ph.D., graduated from the Institute of Transpersonal Psychology. She paints in oils, watercolor, collage, and encaustic and makes commercial decoupage vases and art cards. Her book, *Heal Abuse and Trauma Through Art: Increasing Self-worth, Healing of Initial Wounds, and Creating a Sense of Connectivity*, is the result of doctoral research that explores the connection between the expression of creativity and one's physical, mental, emotional and spiritual health. She is the past President of the National League of American Pen Women, Orlando/Winter Park Branch, and current National Art Chair for new members in the same organization. Her studio is in Tavares, FL.

A.E. Stallings studied classics in Athens, Georgia, and has lived in Athens, Greece since 1999. She has published two collections, *Archaic Smile* (University of Evansville Press, 1999) and *Hapax* (Triquarterly Books, 2005), and a verse translation of Lucretius, *The Nature of Things* (Penguin Classics, 2007).

Timothy Steele is the author of four collections of poetry: *Uncertainties and Rest* (1979), *Sapphics against Anger and Other Poems* (1986), *The Color Wheel* (Johns Hopkins University Press, 1994), and *Toward the Winter Solstice* (Swallow Press/Ohio University Press, 2006). The first two were reprinted as a joint volume, *Sapphics and Uncertainties: Poems 1970-1986* (University of Arkansas Press, 1995). His two books of literary criticism and scholarship are *Missing Measures: Modern Poetry and the Revolt against Meter* (University of Arkansas Press, 1990) and *All the Fun's in How You Say a Thing: An Explanation of Meter and Versification* (Ohio University Press, 1999). He has also edited *The Poems of J. V. Cunningham* (Swallow Press/Ohio University Press, 1997).

David Stephenson graduated from the Massachusetts Institute of Technology and from the University of Wisconsin with degrees in engineering. His work has appeared in *California Quarterly*, *Edge City Review*, *The Formalist*, *Hellas*, *The Lyric*, *Pivot*, and *Slant*. He lives in Detroit, Michigan.

Alan Sullivan was born on August 14, 1948, in Brooklyn, NY. His poetry and essays have appeared in numerous periodicals, including *Poetry*, *Chronicles*, and *The Hudson Review*. He co-translated with Timothy Murphy *Beowulf, A Longman Cultural Edition* (Longman, 2007). He died on July 9, 2010 in Aventura, FL.

Marilyn L. Taylor is the author of six collections of poetry, with the most recent titled *Going Wrong* (Parallel Press, 2009). Her work has also appeared in many anthologies and journals, including *The American Scholar*, *Poetry*, *Valparaiso Review*, *Measure*, *Mezzo Cammin*, and *The Raintown Review*. She taught poetry and poetics at the University of Wisconsin-Milwaukee for many years, and currently serves as a Contributing Editor for *The Writer* magazine, where her columns on craft appear bimonthly. She was appointed Poet Laureate of the State of Wisconsin for 2009 and 2010.

Diane Thiel is the author of nine books of poetry, nonfiction and creative writing pedagogy, including *Echolocations* and *Resistance Fantasies*. Her translation of Alexis Stamatis's novel, *American Fugue*, received an NEA International Literature Award. Her work appears in many journals, is re-printed in over fifty anthologies, and has been translated widely. She has received numerous awards, including the Robert Frost and Robinson Jeffers Awards, a PEN Translation Award, and was a Fulbright Scholar. She is a Writer-in Residence at Sewanee this year, is on the faculty of the Sewanee School of Letters summer MFA program, and is a Professor at the University of New Mexico.

Kamil Varga was born in 1962 in Štúrovo, Slovakia. He is a leading Slovak photographer, specializing in staged photography. He studied at the School of Applied Arts Kosice, Slovakia, and the Prague Academy of Performing Arts (Department of Art Photography). For over 35 years, he has held exhibitions in several galleries including London, Vienna, Berlin, and Hamburg. His photos are stored in museums of fine arts of several European countries. He is the subject of the books, *Kamil Varga-Špirály* by Lucia Benická (1993), and *Kamil Varga* by Václav Macek (1997).

Richard Wakefield teaches writing and American Literature at Tacoma Community College and the University of Washington-Tacoma. For over twenty years he was literary critic for the *Seattle Times*. His collection of poetry, *East of Early Winters*, received the 2006 Richard Wilbur Award, and his poem "Petrarch" won the 2010 Howard Nemerov Sonnet Award. His poetry, criticism, and fiction has appeared in *Sewanee Review*, *American Literature*, *The Midwest Quarterly*, *Atlanta Review*, *Seattle Review*, *Light*, and many others.

Deborah Warren's poetry collections are: *The Size of Happiness* (Waywiser, 2003), runner-up for the 2000 T.S. Eliot Prize; *Zero Meridian*, which received the 2003 New Criterion Poetry Prize (Ivan R. Dee, 2004); and *Dream With Flowers and Bowl of Fruit*, which received the Richard Wilbur Award (University of Evansville, 2008). Her poems have appeared in *The New Yorker*, *The Paris Review*, *Poetry*, and *The Yale Review*.

Bob Watts grew up in rural North Carolina and holds the Creative Writing Ph.D. in English from the University of Missouri-Columbia. His poems have appeared in *Poetry*, *The Paris Review*, *New York Quarterly*, *The Southeast Review*, and other journals. His first collection, *Past Providence*, won the 2004 Stanzas Prize from David Robert Books. He teaches creative writing as a Professor of Practice at Lehigh University.

Robert West's poems, essays, and book reviews have appeared in *Christian Science Monitor*, *Pembroke Magazine*, *Poetry*, *Southern Poetry Review*, *Tar River Poetry*, and other venues. He is the author of two poetry chapbooks, *Best Company* (2005) and *Out of Hand* (2007), and the book review editor of the scholarly journal *Mississippi Quarterly: The Journal of Southern Cultures*. He teaches at Mississippi State University.

Gail White is the author of *Easy Marks* (David Robert Books, 2008), a finalist for the Poets Prize in 2008. She coedited the anthology *The Muse Strikes Back*, which has been reissued by Story Line Press. She is also the subject of Julie Kane's essay "Getting Serious About Gail White's Light Verse", which appeared in an early issue of *Mezzo Cammin*. She lives in Breaux Bridge, Louisiana.

Christopher Woods is a writer, teacher and photographer who lives in Houston and in Chappell Hill, Texas. He has published a prose collection, *Under a Riverbed Sky*, and a collection of stage monologues, *Heart Speak*. His photographs recently appeared, or will appear, in *Anderbo*, *Bap Quarterly*, *Public Republic*, *Glasgow Review* and *Narrative Magazine*. He shares a gallery with his wife, Linda, at Moonbird Hill Arts.

INDEX

217196LV00003B/4/P
LaVergne, TN USA
18 February 2011